T0361308

Virtual Reality and Artificial Intelligence

Technology is rapidly transforming the way people learn and train, and the integration of virtual reality (VR) and artificial intelligence (AI) could be the next big breakthrough. With the advent of Web 3.0 and the Metaverse, there are endless possibilities for creating immersive and engaging learning environments. However, there is also a need to address the risks and challenges that these technologies present.

This book explores the risks and opportunities of VR and AI for coaching and training, with an eye toward the emerging trends of Web 3.0 and the Metaverse. Coaching and training have become increasingly important for companies seeking to develop and retain talent. With the advent of VR and AI technology, there is an opportunity to create immersive and engaging learning environments that could greatly enhance the learning experience. However, there are also risks associated with the use of these technologies, such as data privacy and cybersecurity.

This book provides an in-depth analysis of the risks and opportunities of VR and AI for coaching and training, to help startup and business executives understand how to use these technologies responsibly and effectively. We need a new perspective. The book discusses the intersection of various major subjects and topics: business, innovation, technology, and philosophy in terms of critical thinking. The transition we are experiencing through this new Intelligent Revolution is very important, and soon everyone will witness the shift from e-learning to v-learning.

Virtual Reality and Artificial Intelligence

Risks and Opportunities for Your Business

Matteo Zaralli

Routledge
Taylor & Francis Group
A PRODUCTIVITY PRESS BOOK

First published 2024
by Routledge
605 Third Avenue, New York, NY 10158

and by Routledge
4 Park Square, Milton Park, Abingdon, Oxon, OX14 4RN

Routledge is an imprint of the Taylor & Francis Group, an informa business

© 2024 Matteo Zaralli

The right of Matteo Zaralli to be identified as author of this work has been asserted by him in accordance with sections 77 and 78 of the Copyright, Designs and Patents Act 1988.

All rights reserved. No part of this book may be reprinted or reproduced or utilised in any form or by any electronic, mechanical, or other means, now known or hereafter invented, including photocopying and recording, or in any information storage or retrieval system, without permission in writing from the publishers.

Trademark notice: Product or corporate names may be trademarks or registered trademarks, and are used only for identification and explanation without intent to infringe.

ISBN: 9781032575056 (hbk)
ISBN: 9781032575049 (pbk)
ISBN: 9781003439691 (ebk)

DOI: 10.4324/9781003439691

Typeset in Garamond
by Deanta Global Publishing Services, Chennai, India

Contents

PART IV LEVERAGING YOUR BUSINESS

Foreword

Today's workers shall ignore the potential training application of augmented reality (AR), virtual reality (VR), and artificial intelligence (AI) technologies at their own risk.

The Labor Productivity Conundrum

Organisation for Economic Co-operation and Development (OECD) data on wage trends as compared to those of productivity from 1995 to 2013 have shown a surprising and altogether worrisome phenomenon. During that time period, recorded increases in labor productivity did not coincide with likewise increases in average wages. Economists have described this phenomenon as "decoupling." We know from economic theory that, in general, an increase in labor productivity should be followed by the same kind of increase in wages. Yet this time, it simply did not happen.

It is easy to find the root causes of such a discrepancy. In two recent studies by Gartner (2018 and 2020), out of more than 7.5 million job advertisements in IT, finance, and sales, an average of 17 required skills emerged. This number has risen to 21 today for the same types of employment. On the other hand, 29% of the skills required back in 2018 will no longer be necessary starting next year, the labor market as a whole has dictated.

Even if this highly competitive labor market may require an ever-increasing number of skills, we confirm with dismay that a good number of people in the workforce today are less and less prepared to keep up with such high market demands (Gartner Group, 2020 Stamford, Conn., August 19, 2020, https://www.gartner.com/en/newsroom/press-releases).

Education and Training as a Major Solution

It is self-evident today, as it ever was, that education and training are indispensable tools for avoiding the phenomenon of long-term unemployment in large pockets of the population. Companies should do their part in "reskilling" (developing one's skills to fill a different role) and "upskilling" (upgrading the worker's existing set of skills) since any firm's competitiveness may be at stake if such training activities are not carried out in a consistent and pervasive manner (Pieraccini, I. 2021). But what is going on with regard to corporate training activities and how effective are they at present?

Another Gartner Group study (Skills Shifting Survey) that involved interviews with 7,300 workers and managers from all over the world arrived at the following conclusions. Survey data indicated that there was little relationship between the skills acquired in the classroom or through virtual training during office hours and the percentage of skills actually used on the job. They even agreed on asserting that structured corporate training is becoming too slow for the evolution of the market. In fact, once company training programs have been created and deployed, the training needs tend to have already changed.

Then, what can we workers and companies operating in competitive sectors do? Workers should update their skills on a regular and systematic basis. Some companies have forums where real training needs are discussed and then, swiftly conveyed to the Human Resources department to become actionable (Sari Wilde, Alison Smith, and Sara Clark 2021, HBR). Some of these enlightened firms have established "connectors," employees purposely appointed with the task of alerting them to changes in the structure of skills required for the various types of corporate work.

May AI and VR Come to the Rescue?

To that end, there are highly immersive technologies such as VR and AR that can offer contents and methods, immediately available at work with a significant gain in understanding and memorization for the training participants.

It is true that this would not solve the problem of workers being left by the wayside by the continuous evolution of work skills, but it would increase the way and the effectiveness of learning routines themselves. In reality, the ability to adapt to a constantly changing work environment becomes an ace in the hole for any worker. The ability to build empathy toward others, exercise leadership by enacting personal initiatives in the workplace, and independently improve the quality of work are all traits that prove fundamental in a globalized market like that of today.

Generative AI Breaks Loose

Since the launch of ChatGPT (Generative Pretrained Transformer) at the end of November 2022, a historical marker has been broken. One million users signed up for the service in less than five days. It should be noted that it took Instagram 2.5 months to reach such a level (*The Guardian*). And the record continues today: as of the end of April, there are more than 100 million users and 1.8 billion monthly visitors to the site ChatGPT (Statista, 2023). More than 80% of the system's users access the software through the official Open AI site.

A new generation of AI programs belongs to the category of "machine learning" systems as they piggyback on the successes of ChatGPT. Other generative AI systems are Google Bard, Microsoft Bing Chat, Jasper AI, Meet Claude, ChatSonic, NeevaAi, YouChat, Perplexity, Character.AI, and Elicit among others. Generative AI can "learn" without the direct guidance of human beings. ChatGPT is used for text while Dell-E operates with images (McKinsey Quarterly, Feb. 2023).

Hear It from the Horse's Mouth

In order to illustrate both the relevance and limitations of such systems, we have run a test by asking ChatGPT the following question:

"Will teaching the efficient use of ChatGPT report writing represent a valuable opportunity for professional training improvement?" The system responded "yes." When asked to mention the specific areas where such improvements shall take place, it pointed out the ensuing categories:

1. *Language refinement*: meaning that the use of generative AI can help improve vocabulary by concocting different sentence structures and improved grammar and syntax.
2. *Structure and organization*: generative AI can also help provide titles, and headings which in turn can improve text organization.

3. *Content generation*: the program can help improve text arguments by providing brainstorming, and conceptual improvement in some sections of a given report. It can also provide statistics and data points, and examples to make for a much stronger argumentation rendering the text much clearer.
4. *Summarization and abstract writing*: generative AI can not only provide a summary of the topic but also write short abstracts. This type of feature can save significant amounts of search and correction time.
5. *Formatting and styling*: generative AI can also provide suggestions in terms of bettering format font size, bullets, and quotes to match a specific professional decor.
6. *Data analysis and visualization*: the system can also provide hints for data analysis as well as for data visualization. It can likewise provide interpretation and tips regarding the use of statistical techniques and data visualization tools.
7. *Revision and editing*: generative AI can provide support in spotting sections that need clarification, unclear sentence structure, or simply writing errors.

The Current Debate

There is a heated debate taking place in the media and political realm at large (EU institutions and US Congress) which finds two opposing positions. On the one hand, there are those who hail AI's gains in productivity and efficiency. The opposing side is concerned with major job displacement and swaths of growing number of unemployed workers.

While jobs being displaced are those related to content writing, data entry, assembly line work, bookkeeping, legal advice, language translation, and image analysis, others are probably witnessing growing demand. We are referring to data analysis and interpretation as well as AI programming jobs.

New laws are being debated in the US and EU to curb the negative effects of AI and automation in numerous industries as evidenced in job loss. Although none of them has been formalized yet there are a number of measures that incentivize the private sector to promote on-the-job education and training programs.

Although most policymakers in the EU and US agree that the widespread use of AI will yield productivity and economic gains, job displacement and poverty in large areas of the population are of relentless concern.

A Final Thought

Workers these days must be their own "connectors." Paradoxically, in a competitive working environment with a continuous redefinition of tasks and work objectives, the development of soft skills becomes fundamental (Pieraccini, I. 2021). Extensive literature agrees on indicating that soft skills carry an important key to professional success (Griffiths & Hoppner, 2013; Lazarus, 2013; Seetha, 2014). The advent of generative AI is only emphasizing the importance of these skills even more.

For these reasons, it is highly recommended that workers of today and tomorrow have a good knowledge of the possibilities provided by immersive technologies (VR, AR, and AI) already available in the market at competitive rates. As we have discussed, current workers must become self-promoters and carefully take care of the development of their own technical and relational (soft) skills. The more they do it, the more competitive they shall be in the labor market and the more economic satisfaction they will derive from their daily toil. The risk is that not doing so will leave them out of the market for a very long time.

John Steven Wyse
June 15, 2023

Acknowledgments

To my family who always support me.

To the people who are collaborating on the Vrainers project, Francesco Palazzo and Sebastiano Alvaro, for that fantastic help during those years.

To my friends Walter and Tiziano.

To Prof. Wyse for the Foreword.

To Davide Bartolani for our philosophical conversations.

To all the mentors and wonderful people I have been fortunate to meet and share this path: Alessandro, Alberto, and Eric.

To all founders that contributed to the new, innovative, and pioneering of this market: Gabriele Sorrento, founder of Mindesk; Elia D'Anna and Joseph D'Anna, founders of Veeso.

About the Author

Matteo Zaralli is the founder of VRAINERS, an innovative project that realized an E-learning Platform App in Virtual Reality available on the Meta Quest Store. In 2022, he was the winner of the Fulbright scholarship for the BEST program in California. He worked for StartX in Palo Alto as Communications Fellow. Matteo was the winner of the Intercultura (AFS) scholarship for international school and cultural exchanges. He holds a BSc in Business Administration, an MSc in Management from the European School of Economics, and an MSc in Philosophy from the Università degli studi Roma TRE. As a strategic learning expert, in 2019, he was hosted by RAI1 at the program called "Superbrain," and in 2020, he was hosted by RAI1 at the program called "I soliti ignoti."

Introduction

This book examines how virtual reality (VR) and artificial intelligence (AI) reshape coaching and training. It explores these technologies' risks, opportunities, and philosophical principles. The book covers theoretical and technical aspects, the interplay between human and AI, the transformative power of VR, and real-world case studies. The book highlights the need to understand and navigate this technological wave while emphasizing the importance of human values and creativity. It showcases how VR and AI enhance public speaking, communication, and mindfulness skills. The book concludes with insights into the future of coaching and the synergy between humans and machines. Overall, it provides a concise and comprehensive exploration of how VR and AI revolutionize the coaching and training landscape.

Are VR and AI changing the coaching and training world? What information do we need to deal with this new wave of technology? What are the hidden risks and opportunities?

The world is evolving. The skills required were only technical, known as "hard skills"; then it was noticed that the most successful people and entrepreneurs had additional skills, known as "soft skills." What do we need?

These are the issues this book aims to bring up—theoretical and technical considerations on the one hand and critical and philosophical aspects on the other.

The book is divided into four parts. The first part encapsulates the basics of understanding from a theoretical and technical perspective of how we got here today, starting with an analysis of new trends, with the help of charts published by the Gartner Group, and then moving on to technological progress and this new smart revolution. VR, augmented reality, and AI spotlight through critical and opportunity considerations for an expanding market. In the end, the first part closes with a new emerging figure that I coined the term "A Super Artificial Worker," that is, a person who works equipped with new empowering tools, such as those of AI that enhance its speed, while at the same time threatening to undermine so many other jobs. An in-depth look at AI, how it was born, who the first people to talk about it are, and how we have gone from a "winter AI" to a real gold rush; in this case, a race for AI.

The second part, as anticipated at the beginning, opens the door to critical philosophical and technical issues. We are faced with a challenge between human intelligence and AI. What are the differences between the two? In what areas can we use AI and in what tasks does it fail to over-power human uniqueness? Critical reflections help us understand that although we may have powerful tools, we cannot "turn off our minds" and entrust everything to a machine. Our values, decision-making scale, cre-ativity, imagination, consciousness, and emotional intelligence are part of a holistic system that scientists and researchers are currently studying.

The openness of data-driven technologies brings new issues, such as data security, ethical and legal problems, adopting new technologies in the enter-prise, and return on costs. A further thought was learned and confirmed during Silicon Valley, namely the three new skills we need today: business, tech, and philosophy.

The third part addresses an in-depth analysis of why VR changes how we learn, study, and process information. What is the difference between passive learning and active learning? How can VR, with the support and enhancement of AI, realize virtual learning by doing?

Over the years, mainly thanks to Covid-19, the digitization process has been accelerated; digital training, so all those activities that used to be done in person, has now been made accessible to everyone thanks to video courses. The e-learning market has exponentially increased, as has the era of digital business. In recent years, online activities have exploded with the emergence of a new figure, the digital nomad. VR and AI are the next steps. We are entering the era of Coaching and Training 3.0.

The fourth and final part reports real, practical examples with case stud-ies from companies innovating the coaching and training world. In par-ticular, how can public speaking, communication, mindfulness, creativity, and many other skills be coached and enhanced through VR and AI? There are several topics in particular: developing soft skills in VR, such as public speaking, communication, emotional intelligence, leadership, decision-mak-ing, problem-solving, and resilience. The second aspect is accessibility to new analytics data to accelerate the coaching process, predictive ability, and privacy and ethics considerations.

Part IV closes with a perspective on the future of coaching with new case studies and companies currently in the international market, and a new concept of synergy between man and machine.

The book concludes by analyzing two quotes from two significant historical figures: Steve Jobs and Winston Churchill, commenting and analyzing why some of their quotes are truer today than ever.

Technology is advancing at lightning speed, and staying ahead in business has never been more challenging. As an entrepreneur or manager, you know that success hinges on understanding and anticipating the market.

You will explore four essential parts. First, gain a deep understanding of new technologies and their potential. Then delve into critical topics like ethics and the future of humanity. Next, discover how to leverage these technologies to your advantage in business. Finally, uncover the risks we face and learn to navigate them.

Packed with graphs, case studies, and insights from Silicon Valley founders, this book is your indispensable guide to thriving in today's rapidly evolving landscape. Accelerate your success and seize the opportunities of technology and business.

THE INTELLIGENT REVOLUTION

Chapter 1

At This Speed, Where Will We Go?

The chosen theme is related to different and meaningful worlds: training and personal growth and the world of innovation.

Companies are developing VR for training, and there are many new applications with these technologies, such as in the industrial sector, where people train with visors to reduce time and risks at work. The combination of VR and AR allows the opening of new businesses, such as architecture, where it is possible to give a different perspective of a building. Thanks to AR and VR, people who want to build a new house can see their ideas and projects in 3D format and better understand what they want and how they want to achieve it.

Mark Zuckerberg announced the new Meta project, a virtual or AR parallel universe called "Metaverse." They are trying to replicate what is seen in "Ready Player One." It is a recommended film, but it is fair to consider this hypothesis and hope we stay within that point, given the market and companies running.

Another vital area that is changing so much is marketing. How a product will be sold and displayed: let us think of the stores where it is possible to buy glasses that have incorporated the function of AR. Thanks to a touch mirror, clients can select the model of the glasses, the color, and the shape and virtually test them—an exciting experience and worth trying.

Moreover, a new market to study and understand is non-fungible token (NFT) and crypto. It is not only to be learned but also well understood since the world of Metaverse, NFT, and crypto will be one shoulder to the other.

These chapters' protagonists are changing how a specific product will be tested, perceived, and sold.

DOI: 10.4324/9781003439691-2

Getting more specific in the training industry, many companies have already started to benefit from some great features; for example, Walmart has incorporated VR for their employees, and other companies are doing the same. In the medical industry, surgeons use these tools to improve surgical procedures and save more lives.

At the same time, new apps are taking over our lives, like Siri or Alexa: before users knew these names, they probably saw someone on the street asking questions or various types of information on their phones but did not realize what happened. This type of technology is known as artificial intelligence (AI) and is based on machine learning programmed to develop specific features of languages. This field has many applications, and people are still improving ways to empower this technology.

Now, after these small introductions to the subject, which we will shortly go into in more detail, it is good to bring attention to some reflections: Why don't we use these new technological tools to improve our daily lives? Why not develop soft skills? How can we connect the world of training and human skills development with these new technologies?

In Harari's book *21 Lessons for the 21st Century*, at the end of the first chapter, the author writes,

> the technological revolution could, in a short time, oust billions of human beings from the labor market and create a huge new class of useless individuals, causing social and political upheavals for which no ideology can control the consequences. The whole technological and ideological discourse may sound abstract and remote, but the real prospect of mass unemployment—or individual unemployment—leaves no one indifferent.

To date, Harari continues, humans should put themselves at the service of AI and not compete with it to fully exploit its potential:

> in fact, there is no need to fear that AI may become conscious because intelligence and consciousness are distinct phenomena. Intelligence is the ability to solve problems. Consciousness is feeling things like fear, joy, love, and anger. The risk is that if we invest too much in the development of AI and too little in the development of human consciousness, the very sophisticated AI of computers might only empower the natural stupidity of human beings.

Answering this is not easy, much less finding a solution. Still, we can analyze what research and studies are bringing out about VR and AI, and then try to match them with what human abilities encompass and all the tools we use today to implement our capabilities (Harari & Piani, 2020).

In the book *Dawn of the New Everything*, Lanier reports this definition of VR,

> one of the scientific, philosophical and technological frontiers of our age. A means of creating illusions so complete that you believe you are in a different place, perhaps a fantastic, alien place, with a body that has nothing human. However, at the same time, technology allows you to understand better what a human being is cognitively and perceptually.

It is relevant to analyze two Gartner curves, one from 2020 and the second from 2022, and see the differences.

Starting in 2020, they organized over 1,700 new technologies into five main trends: composer architecture, algorithms trust, beyond silicon, formative AI, and digital me.

Formative AI is artificial intelligence that can change dynamically to respond to a situation. There are various models ranging from AI that can dynamically adapt over time to technologies that can generate new processes to solve specific problems. This new tool could hint at a negative impact, i.e., being able to create "fake" content capable of creating misinformation or even burdening it from a "reputational" standpoint (Gartner, 2020).

These were the predictions for 2020. Now we gaze toward the study also conducted by Gartner in 2022.

Within the article, Gartner highlights three essential themes:

1. Evolving/expansion immersive experiences
2. Accelerated AI automation
3. Optimized technologist delivery

Let us start with the first point. These technologies are advantageous because they provide people more control over their identities and data and broaden their variety of experiences by allowing them to participate in virtual environments and ecosystems that can be combined with digital currencies. These technologies also offer fresh ways to connect with clients to expand or create new revenue streams.

The technologies are:

■ Decentralized identity
■ Digital humans

- Internal talent marketplaces
- Metaverse
- Non-fungible token
- Superapp
- Web3

The graph represents 2022, but 2023 began with two robust technologies vying for the market. We saw Mark Zuckerberg change the name of his company to Meta to launch the Metaverse. Conversely, ChatGPT sparked a gold rush.

The critical technologies mentioned by Gartner are:

- Causal AI
- Foundation models
- Generative design AI
- Machine learning code generation

The third theme is the optimized technologist delivery. These technologies concentrate on the communities of people that create products, services, and solutions. These technologies offer feedback and insight that improve the delivery of goods, services, and solutions.

- Augmented FinOps
- Cloud sustainability
- Computational storage (CS)
- Cybersecurity mesh architecture (CSMA)
- Data observability
- Dynamic risk governance (DRG)
- Industry cloud platform
- Minimum valuable architecture (MVA)
- Observability-driven development (ODD)
- Open telemetry
- Platform engineering

All those new trends can represent opportunities and risks for businesses at the same time. Entrepreneurs can understand how to innovate and implement recent trends within their companies (Gartner, 2022).

AI is the most disruptive technology, and although it is driving benefits for early "adapters" due to the continued evolution of the technology, it will be a significant and complex change for the population. At the same time, it is fostering developers, data scientists, and AI architecture to create new and compelling solutions (Gartner, 2020). We can also see that virtual assistants' productivity plateau will be reached in 2 to 5 years, and mixed reality and AR in 5 to 10 years. Above all, AR is moving from the Trough of Disillusionment to the Slope of Enlightenment.

With the cooperation of these new technologies, it is possible to give a more incredible feeling of resemblance to humans through a virtual avatar and create a real conversation as if we were talking to someone. The benefits are obvious; people will be more independent in terms of time and space to learn and develop new skills and improve their quality at work.

However, as with all new technologies and innovations, there are the same positives and negatives; people need to be aware of both.

Soft skills are even more critical. However, we are moving toward a future where robots and intelligent machines will probably replace most of our jobs (Ross, 2016).

As also anticipated by psychologist Luca Mazzucchelli, we are in the age of the heart, an era in which machines will overtake mechanical, repetitive, or intellectual jobs, while what machines or AI find difficult to replicate today is our emotions.

Let us look at some graphs to understand the approximate market developments in virtual intelligence, augmented intelligence, and AI (Figure 1.1) (Statista, 2021).

The VR and AR market is growing year by year, and as we can see from the graph, it will reach $52.05 billion by 2027. According to the article published by Statista, the data represent only the B2C revenue covered by the market.

Thanks to Meticulous Research, the "speech and voice recognition" market is expected to reach $26.79 billion by 2025. We can see the first examples. We have seen the advertising of the new Lavazza coffee machine with Alexa.

The recent head-mounted displays (HMD) VR, such as HTC Vive, Oculus Rift, and recently on the market Oculus Quest 2 and Oculus Pro, allow users an increasingly immersive and realistic experience. Due to the immersive experience and involvement within the virtual environment, awareness of time and the natural world is almost lost. The VR system engages the user through images, sounds, and other stimuli. According to the report published by Global Augmented Reality, the HMD market is expected to be valued at $25 billion by 2022, growing at a Compound Annual Growth Rate (CAGR) of 39.52% between 2019 and 2025. With continued study and research, we have arrived at an HMD, like the Oculus Quest 2 today is "standalone," i.e., wireless, at a favorable price point and certainly a step up from the Rift. Furthermore, VR has been described as the learning aid of the 21st century (Figure 1.2).

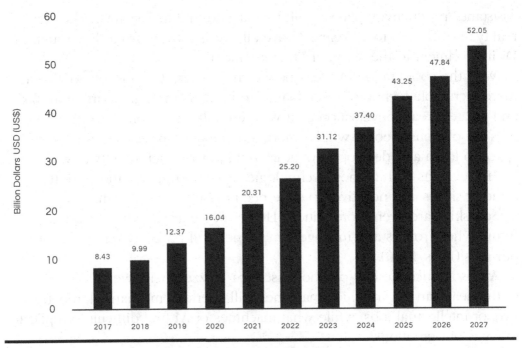

Figure 1.1   AR and VR worldwide. Personal elaboration.

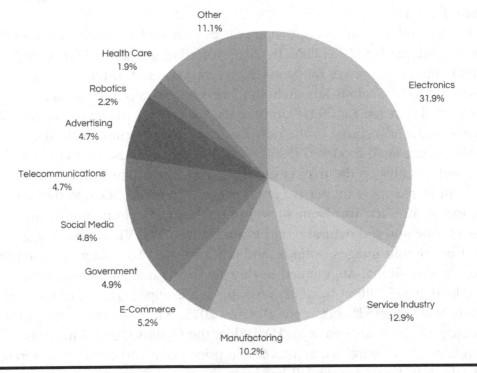

Figure 1.2   Revenue shared per industry. Personal elaboration.

This book aims to understand how these technologies work, how their combination can be to our advantage, how they can be used to develop human capabilities in the coaching sector, and where machines cannot replace humans.

References

Gartner (2020). *5 trends drive the Gartner Hype Cycle for Emerging Technologies, 2020*. Gartner. Available at: https://www.gartner.com/smarterwithgartner/5 -trends-drive-the-gartner-hype-cycle-for-emerging-technologies-2020/.

Gartner (2022). *What is new in the 2022 Gartner Hype Cycle for Emerging Technologies*. Gartner. Available at: https://www.gartner.com/en/articles/what-s -new-in-the-2022-gartner-hype-cycle-for-emerging-technologies.

Harari, Y., & Piani, M. (2020). *21 lezioni per il XXI secolo*, 19–120. Milan: Bompiani.

Ross, A. (2016). *The industries of the future*. Simon & Schuster.

Statista. (2021). *VR/AR market size | Statista*. [online] Available at: https://www. statista.com/statistics/591181/global-augmented-virtual-reality-market-size/.

Chapter 2

Technological Progress

Technology has profoundly changed our lives, especially in the last two decades. The advent of the internet and PCs, cell phones first, and then smartphones has changed our daily habits, leading us to connect for many hours of the day constantly. On the one hand, we see positive effects, such as greater access to information and the opportunities it offers in different areas of our existence. At the same time, technological evolution can have adverse effects. "Technology should enhance your life, not become your life." The statement of this well-known American entrepreneur sums up the phenomenon we are witnessing nowadays, namely "a hyper-digitalization of our daily lives." So, an essential aspect of technology that has attracted increasing interest is the relationship between man and computer. The latter is a constant interaction that has changed our communication, behaviors, and reality. The Canadian sociologist Marshall McLuhan (1967) has highlighted how fundamental it is to study the structural organization of technology and its peculiarities in terms of content disseminated and communication modes. Technological tools are also identified with the name of *digital media* to highlight the phenomenon of digitalization mentioned above.

The term "technology" has changed significantly over the past 200 years. Before the 20th century, the term was unusual in the English language. It usually refers to the description or study of technique, which is "the application of knowledge developed by science to practical purposes and to the production of tools to accomplish them." Several sociologists have been interested in this area, beginning to make technology coincide with the technical subjects themselves. They arrive at a definition that most scholars still agree with: "Technology includes all tools, machines, utensils, weapons, musical

 DOI: 10.4324/9781003439691-3

instruments, dwellings, clothing, communication and transportation devices, and the skill by which we produce and use these things." More generally, the term technology is often associated with science, primarily because the scientific method lays the groundwork for validating effective techniques. In reality, technology is a product of science, and at the same time, the former is not necessarily based on purely scientific models (think of the technology of glass production). Technology comprises "mediums," i.e., means of communication, which have undergone an important evolution in their mode of interaction with man. Today we talk about "new media" and not "new mediums" because we refer to technological tools that are different from each other and have dynamic structures that are unstable or fixed, which tend to merge. With the concept of "medium," we refer to "any tool (artifact) capable of allowing subjects to overcome the constraints of face-to-face communication, the most natural interactive situation." Therefore, these tools are fundamental because they act as mediation devices in the relationship. On the one hand, they do nothing but make communication more effective by going beyond the limits of face-to-face interaction. On the other hand, it becomes a mediated experience (a real experience replaced with an indirect/mediated perception). Man is a social being: social interaction is an important protection factor since it decreases the probability of developing discomfort or disorders, is a source of well-being, and improves self-esteem and a sense of control over one's life. Through it, we share a language, a culture, and always thanks to social relations, we understand ourselves and our aspirations. Our social network can influence our attitudes, which affect the implementation of certain behaviors. Technological evolution led to the transition from analog (older) to digital (new) media. The former uses an analog representation, i.e., a phenomenon that is described continuously, while the latter uses the modern approach of digital representation, a discontinuous phenomenon. As already anticipated, this great change derived from technological evolution has disrupted our lives and changed how we communicate. In this regard, telecommunications systems have undergone a "digitalization" process. There has been a shift from analog to digital television and the cell phone, whose contents have become increasingly extended (images, sounds, videos, video games, and the internet). The press has now been surpassed in some ways, thanks to the creation of e-books capable of containing thousands of books that can be consulted on computer devices without carrying around the physical object (the book). So technology has tried to satisfy some requests to facilitate the user's life, focusing on easy accessibility through different devices. In addition, as with the e-book, there is a separation between technology and content (there is no longer physical support for the content) and the use of corporeality to make the interaction with the new media as similar as possible to that with the real environment (interactivity). From what can be deduced from the preceding lines, these tools have evolved so much that scholars have come to speak of *new media*. The aspect that strongly distinguishes the "mediums" of the past from the more recent ones is the coding language they use: the former use analog coding, while the latter uses digital coding. Analog representation identifies a continuous phenomenon: for example, the continuous movement of the second hand indicates the passage of time. The digital representation, however, identifies a discontinuous phenomenon: an example is a digital clock, according to which a succession of clicks marks the passage of time. Intuitively, one might think that the first is more accurate than the second, but it is not always so; if we take as an example the clocks, the digital one, in addition to scanning the passage of seconds, can also report the passage of tenths and hundredths of a second, which the automatic clock is not able to do (analog). Most information used to be transmitted in analog format, while today, with the innovation of tools, we are increasingly moving to digital. *New media* paves the way for a trend presented earlier, namely interactivity. Interactivity, about a computer application, is

> the ability of the user to modify the content displayed on the monitor or the sound coming from the speakers through a series of motor actions on an interface. The more motor activity that takes place in an environment that simulates interaction with a world with characteristics similar to the real world, the greater the feeling of interactivity.
>
> **(Grodal, 2003)**

So from this definition, we can understand that these tools allow the user to enjoy the content actively, interacting with it on a freeway.

By now, it is clear that technologies are part of our everyday life, and their use is increasing more and more. New media are accused of creating dependency, cooling human relationships, triggering negative social dynamics, depowering writing and reading processes, and, last but not least, impoverishing learning processes. Starting from this, the need to investigate the positive effects of the use of technology has developed to highlight the great potential of the *new media* both on a cognitive, emotional, and social level. It is in this sense that *Positive Technology* was born, defined as "an applied scientific approach that uses technology to modify the characteristics of our personal experience—structuring it, augmenting it or replacing it with synthetic environments—to improve its quality and increase well-being in individuals, organizations, and societies" (Riva et al., 2006). This discipline's theoretical frame of reference is positive psychology, which focuses on individuals' strengths and resources by enhancing them and promoting social empowerment and individual development (Seligman and Csitksentmihaly, 2000). Another essential contribution at the theoretical level, which flows into positive technology, is cognitive psychology, dedicated to studying mental processes involved in subjective experience (perception, memory, reasoning, and thinking). The structuring of the new discipline oriented on the beneficial effects of technologies starts from a fundamental study that has closely related positive psychology with the study of cognitive processes. Martin Seligman stated that it achieves optimal functioning on an individual and social level; it is necessary to refer to three essential aspects of *good living* (Seligman, 2002):

■ an enjoyable life, which is achieved through the experience of positive emotions;

■ engaging energy, which is achieved through involvement in rewarding activities;

■ a meaningful life, which is the pursuit of a more significant burst of self.

From here, it has been inferred that positive functioning is the result of the combination of three types of well-being: emotional well-being (adequate quality), psychological well-being (involvement/self-actualization), and social well-being (relationship and social esteem). We can understand how new technologies can promote development and well-being, thanks to these reflections resulting from the strong connection between these two research areas. Also, according to these scholars, positive technology in the field of application is divided into three different regions: *hedonic technologies*, *eudaimonic technologies*, and *social/interpersonal technologies*.

Hedonic technologies are the first level of positive technologies used to promote positive emotions. The reference model, in this case, according to which it is possible to modify the affective quality of an experience through the manipulation of the "core affect," a primary affective state given by the combination of the five dimensions of activation and valence. It is a fluctuating condition with no object but gives rise to emotion when directed toward a thing. So, this type of technology tries to induce a positive emotional state by modifying the "core effect" (an increase in positive valence and activation level). Examples of this technique are apps that improve stress management and promote relaxation or virtual reality, which we will see later. Eudaimonic technologies are the second level of positive technologies and put individuals in a position to realize engaging and self-fulfilling experiences.

In this case, the reference model is that of *Flow*, developed by the founder of positive psychology, Csikszentmihalyi (1990). The *Flow* or optimal experience is a state of positive awareness experienced in situations of balance between the challenge proposed by the environment (challenge) and the assessment of having the skills to deal with it (skill). Examples of these technologies are those that can help meditation processes or increase awareness of what we are doing, immersive and interactive technologies such as serious games, and in particular, the use of virtual reality as a strategy of "flow transformation" (Riva et al., 2006): to draw from an optimal experience induced by technology and use it to promote new and unexpected psychological resources through a series of activities. Social/interpersonal technologies are the final level to support and enhance social connectedness among individuals, groups, and organizations. The model on which this level is based is that having and maintaining stable and extensive social networks is an essential protective factor for health and increases the likelihood of experiencing greater well-being.

An interesting example is the use of social networking and pervasive computing to help reduce feelings of social isolation and depression in older people (Morris, 2005). All these technologies develop a sense of belonging and create a sense of community even when people are not physically co-present. But on a practical level, how is technology designed? From a technological perspective, positive technology intervenes in the factors that characterize an experience through these new technical means by using them in three different ways (Riva et al., 2006):

■ Structure the experience using a goal, which directs the action of rules, which show alternative views of the experience and feedback to support motivation. Examples of this application method are serious games, persuasive technology, and social media.
■ To "augment" the experience through multisensory, including virtual objects superimposed on real ones. An example of this application is augmented reality.
■ To replace the experience with a synthetic one, which facilitates controllability by the user. In this case, the most used technology is virtual reality.

Suppose we continue to investigate in this sense. In that case, we quickly realize that positive technologies rest on experiential technologies, which, as mentioned earlier, intervene in experience in the different ways just presented with the ultimate goal of intervening in interaction. In fact, through positive technologies, "it is possible to modify a trend of human-computer interaction, making interaction with *new media* as similar as possible to interaction as a real environment" (Riva et al., 2006). These studies have developed a series of research areas that have led to the emergence of technologies that allow the user to make and live an experience, combining the perceptual component with interactivity.

References

Csikszentmihalyi, M. (1990). *Flow: The psychology of optimal experience.* New York, HarperCollins.

McLuhan, M., & Fiore, Q. (1967). *The medium is the massage: An inventory of effects.* New York: Bantam Books.

Morris, M.E. (2005). Social networks as health feedback displays. *IEEE Internet Computing,* 9(5), 29–37.

Riva, G., Castelnuovo, G., & Mantovani, F. (2006). Transformation of flow in rehabilitation: The role of advanced communication technologies. *Behavior Research Methods,* 38(2), 237–44.

Seligman, M.E.P. (2002). *Authentic happiness: Using the new positive psychology to realize your potential for lasting fulfillment.* New York, The Free Press.

Seligman, M., & Csikszentmihalyi, M. (2000). Positive psychology. *American Psychologist,* 55, 5–14.

Chapter 3

The New Web

Why should businesses in the coaching field engage in discussions about the metaverse, NFTs, and crypto? These topics may initially seem overwhelming, but their presence in the coaching industry is becoming increasingly inevitable, given the rapid pace of technological advancements.

The metaverse concept was coined by Neal Stevenson in 1992 in his book *Snow Crash*; it offers a new perspective on the internet in contrast to Web 2.0. As coaches move toward Web 3.0, they must know the potential opportunities and challenges. The metaverse presents a digital realm where coaches can connect with clients, create immersive coaching experiences, and establish their brand presence dynamically and engagingly.

NFTs have gained significant attention in recent times. These unique digital assets enable coaches to tokenize and monetize their coaching programs, courses, or exclusive content. NFTs provide a new revenue stream and can revolutionize how coaches deliver their expertise to a global audience.

On the other hand, cryptocurrencies have become a prominent aspect of the financial landscape. Embracing crypto can offer coaches faster, more secure transactions, lower fees, and the ability to tap into a global market of clients. The underlying technology behind cryptocurrencies, blockchain, also presents opportunities for enhanced transparency and accountability in the coaching industry.

As coaches navigate the evolving digital landscape, it is crucial to understand the implications and possibilities that the metaverse, NFTs, and crypto present. Embracing these technologies can provide a competitive edge, open new revenue streams, and foster innovation in coaching methodologies. By staying informed and proactive, coaches can position themselves for success in the dynamic world of coaching in the 21st century.

DOI: 10.4324/9781003439691-4

The most relevant aspects of Web 3.0 are:

■ semantic web, where we no longer have a page construction in HTML but from an underlying database;
■ artificial intelligence tied to a storage data structure, also taking it a step further, where we will be able to query search engines through natural language;
■ computing power, new algorithms aimed at building truly usable 3D environments, and the evolution of Second Life, the ancestor of the metaverse.

The semantic web will be one of the strong points. AI can decompose sentences and assign roles by explaining more precise semantics to create an honest human–machine dialogue, similar to the Turing test.

The advent of Web 3.0 becomes interesting when the topic of human–computer interaction is included. The consequences will be avatars, animated graphic figures able to dialogue intelligently with the human user.

So why include it in a virtual reality (VR), AI, and human skills discussion?

The answer is simple. Big companies and brands are inserting their brands and securing their place in important metaverses. How? Through NFT. Moreover, how can metaverses be acquired? Through cryptocurrencies.

Let us step back and try to understand what they are and how to fit them within this project.

3.1 Blockchain

Let us start with the definition given by IBM:

> The blockchain is a shared, immutable ledger that facilitates recording transactions and tracking assets in a commercial network. An asset can be tangible (a house, a car, money, land) or intangible (intellectual property, patents, copyrights, branding). Virtually anything of value can be tracked and traded on a blockchain network, reducing risk and cost for all involved.

Blockchain, as well as business, is about information. Today, we are always looking for speed and quality, and blockchain is ideal because it transmits data in an immediate, shared, and transparent way through an immutable ledger that can only be accessed by authorized network members (IBM, 2021).

Let us look at three essential elements of this new technology:

- Distributed log: all participants will have access to the distributed record.
- Immutable records: no one will be able to manipulate or modify a transaction.
- Smart contracts: it is stored automatically.

Blockchain operations:

- when a transaction occurs, it is recorded as a data block: for both tangible and intangible products and can contain any type of data;
- each block is connected to those preceding and following it;
- operations are locked together in an irreversible chain.

3.1.1 Cryptocurrencies

The word can be broken down into two parts: crypto and currency. The currency is "hidden" and visible or usable only by knowing a specific computer code through "access keys." Cryptocurrency is not tangible but virtual, so it is only exchanged electronically, so we will not find, for example, Bitcoins in paper or metal format.

Nowadays, we also talk about virtual wallets, called "wallets" or "e-wallets."

To these concepts must be added another essential principle: coins can be exchanged in a "peer-to-peer" way, that is, between two devices without intermediaries' obligation to purchase goods or services.

Another critical difference is between "closed," "unidirectional," and "bidirectional" virtual currency.

The main difference between the three is the possibility of not exchanging cryptocurrency with official currency. For example, Bitcoin is a bidirectional virtual currency because it can be converted with the main official currencies, and the same thing people can buy Bitcoin with the Euro or other currencies.

3.1.2 NFT

Let us move on to another exciting technology wave already available. NFTs translated means "non-fungible digital token."

Let us start right away with the difference between fungible and non-fungible. Bitcoin can be replaced with another, so we can call it fungible. An NFT, on the other hand, is not because they are unique pieces and cannot be replicated or replaced. An NFT can be a video, a photo, a GIF, a text, an article, or an audio; therefore, a certified digital object as if it had the author's signature on it. Furthermore, NFTs could only exist with the blockchain, which provides a secure and immutable system and ledger to store data transactions (Ferrari & Adonopoulos, 2021).

An example of NFTs is Crypto Art, which has become a race to produce unique pieces of art that, to this day, sell for millions.

Why are people buying NFTs for millions? This is a fundamental blockchain revolution. Whoever buys an NFT is buying the work and claiming a right to claim it. An NFT was sold for $7.6 million.

How to invest in NFT? Several platforms buy and invest in NFT. The Open Sea, the digital currency of exchange, is Ethereum. Other platforms are Raible, SuperRare, and Foundation.

Here is a great challenge and opportunity at the same time for creatives who can not only "vent" their creativity but also increase their economic feedback.

At the same time, we begin to talk about the role of NFTs in the intent of VR, especially in this second virtual world, coined as the metaverse.

3.2 Metaverse

The metaverse was coined for the first time by Neal Stephenson in his book *Snow Crash* in 1992. The novel describes a virtual reality shared through the internet where users can "be present" in three dimensions through avatars.

Then it was the science fiction film *Ready Player One* that brought a representation of the metaverse to our screens for the first time.

In the book *Metaverse* written by Matthew Ball, we can find this definition:

> A highly scalable and interoperable network of real-time rendered 3D virtual worlds, which can be experienced synchronously and persistently by an effectively unlimited number of users with an individual sense of presence within them, and which guarantee the continuity of data on identity, history, rights, objects, communications, and payments. (Ball, 2022)

The metaverse will work through VR and augmented reality (AR) viewers. By wearing them, users will enter a virtual world where they can follow a meeting with colleagues, go shopping, try a new collection of clothing brands, play games, and meet friends.

Inside the metaverse, it will also be possible to buy virtual objects, thanks to blockchain technology and NFTs, such as works of art, sports tokens, and much more. Today, Facebook has changed its name to Meta. Other companies like Microsoft, Roblox, Epic Games, Tencent, Alibaba, and ByteDance have already announced their entry into the metaverse market. It has already announced its entry into the metaverse market by investing millions of dollars.

In the article published by Meta in late October 2021, CEO and Founder Mark Zuckerberg begins his announcement like this:

> We are at the beginning of the next chapter for the internet, and it is the next chapter for our company too.

From the first sentence, we can understand that what is happening is just the beginning. We think about the impact that Facebook has had on our lives, and considering that Facebook over the years has bought Instagram, WhatsApp, and Oculus, we can understand that when such a company makes a decision, its impact on our lives is felt and even strong.

The founder himself describes it this way:

> In the metaverse, you can do almost anything you can imagine—get together with friends and family, work, learn, play, shop, create—and completely new experiences that do not fit how we think about computers or phones today. We made a film that explores how you might use the metaverse one day.

(Meta, 2021)

From this point of view, we can already imagine that the reality we have seen in the movie *Ready Player One* could be just the beginning, since Meta CEO writes: "You will be able to do almost anything you can imagine."

To date, the main problem of the metaverse is not the software, but the hardware, i.e., the usability of the project and the accessibility to the masses. To date, some visors are less accessible than others. Think of MagicLeap or similar products for $4,000 to $5,000. Another important aspect is the management of the metaverse: if companies will manage it, what could be the consequences? If there is something that dictates the rules in a virtual world, how can we rethink free will?

Also, to date already, with social media in recent years, one of the hottest issues, and one that Facebook itself has been under indictment for, is how user data are handled. How will our privacy be managed in a world where the amount of data available will increase? We are just at the beginning, but this is a vital aspect to consider.

Let us go back for a moment instead to the movie set, *Ready Player One*, located in Columbus, Ohio, in 2025, taking apart from the trailer available on YouTube:

> and I ended up here. Here is my little corner of nowhere. Nowhere to go. No one. Except Oasis! A whole virtual universe. People come to Oasis for all they can do, but they stay for all they can be.
>
> **(*Ready Player One*, Italian Trailer)**

There are those who, like Elon Musk, try to take us into space to safeguard the human species and those who, like Mark Zuckerberg, create a second virtual world but leave us on Earth. Another critical point of reflection is that it helps us connect the first points and topics we will discuss in the following chapters.

3.2.1 Features

The characteristics of the metaverse can change based on the situation in which it is employed. However, some of the typical features are as follows:

■ *Immersion*: the metaverse aims to provide people with a compelling alternate reality experience.

■ *Interactivity*: users can engage in dynamic, real-time interactions with each other and the metaverse's material.

■ *Personalization*: by selecting clothing, accessories, and distinguishing features, users can alter their avatars' appearances and surroundings.

■ *Content creation*: user-created content can be shared, edited, and created within the metaverse.

■ *Communication*: the metaverse provides several communication methods, including chat, private messages, and other sorts of contact.

■ *Collaboration*: users can digitally collaborate and exchange content in the metaverse.

■ *Continuity*: the metaverse is a dynamic environment constantly evolving based on user interactions and actions.

3.2.2 Avatar

Avatars represent individuals or fictional characters in online spaces like chat rooms, video games, and virtual worlds. Avatars can be used to engage with other avatars in a virtual environment or to represent the user in online communications.

Avatars can take on a variety of shapes, including those of people or animals, and they can be personalized with clothes, accessories, and distinguishing characteristics. They can convey one's individuality or create a virtual person with traits dissimilar from those of the natural person.

In online games, virtual worlds, and chat rooms, avatars are frequently used to represent users graphically and enable user interaction. Avatars can also be a communication tool in business contexts like online meetings or training sessions.

According to the article published in 2023, "People, places, and time: A large-scale, longitudinal study of transformed avatars and environmental context in group interaction in the Metaverse."

It transformed the Social Interaction paradigm (Bailenson et al., 2004) to examine different avatar identities and environments over time. In Study 1 (n 1/4 81), entitativity, presence, enjoyment, and realism increased over eight weeks. Avatars that resembled participants increased synchrony and similarities in moment-to-moment nonverbal behaviors between participants. Moreover, self-avatars increased self-presence and realism but decreased enjoyment compared to uniform avatars.

Moreover, the presence of an avatar has been demonstrated to boost trust, reduce cognitive burden, and increase social presence, or "the sense of being with another." The impact of psychological distance that may exist between interactants who are physically separated has yet to receive adequate attention from researchers. However, there has been an increase in interest in online learning that incorporates avatar instructors to address this impact (Han et al., 2023).

BOX 3.1: CASE STUDY—METAHUMAN

MetaHuman Creator, a free cloud streaming app, allows for the quick generation of photorealistic and fully customizable virtual humans. Users can select a starting face and freely modify every detail, including facial features, hairstyle, eyebrow shape, color, and skin and teeth details. Epic Games, renowned for games like Gears of War and Fortnite and the widely used Unreal Engine game development toolkit, has developed MetaHuman Creator. Models created with this app can be exported, animated, and utilized within the Unreal Engine. The goal is to reduce production times and costs, which typically require expensive equipment and specialized teams. This creation tool can be used in both the gaming industry and the film industry, often in combination with techniques such as motion capture (recording and digitizing actors' body and facial movements) and rigging (digital animation of a character), to create highly realistic simulations of people and movements. Let us also consider the coaching aspect for a moment. One of the main challenges was using "cartoonish" 3D characters, which are perfect for video games but less suitable for coaching purposes.

3.2.3 Virtual Worlds

Digital spaces that may be explored and navigated using a computer or virtual reality equipment are called virtual worlds and the metaverse, respectively. Virtual worlds are online settings that can be used for various purposes, including gaming, communication, and education. They may have interactive components like user-controlled characters, objects, and activities and may be created to resemble either the real world or a fantastical one.

The term "metaverse" refers to a collection of virtual worlds and the network of links that connects them. The metaverse can be considered a "digital universe" where users can roam between virtual worlds and interact just like in the real world.

BOX 3.2: CASE STUDY—HONG KONG INTERNATIONAL AIRPORT DIGITAL TWIN

General information: Hong Kong International Airport is a commercial airport serving Hong Kong, built on reclaimed land on the island of Chek Lap Kok. The airport has been in commercial operation since 1998. The overall digital strategy for the Airport Authority Hong Kong is to digitize the airport facility, creating a digital twin of the entire 12.5 sq km site. Over 70,000 employees work within the airport facilities.

A development platform designed to integrate and create 3D models, used in video games and architecture, was then used to navigate the 3D model of the airport in a photo-realistic manner. To bring the digital twin to life, the model is linked to real-time data from IoT devices throughout the airport, with simulation tools, corporate applications, and an enterprise analytic platform to enable HKIA to predict what could happen in the future.

In addition to its widespread use in a variety of industries, including gaming, entertainment, training, and education, virtual worlds and the metaverse have the potential to be used as platforms for innovation and cooperation at the corporate level. As with any technology, there are worries about online security and privacy when using these digital spaces.

Moreover, students are likely to be apprehensive, disengaged, and unwilling to take the risks associated with learning without a sense of community. Students might overcome a social threshold and start to feel a sense of belonging in an ideal educational environment while discussing the social aspect of the success of online learning, which is another type of distance education. Teachers can develop a sense of community in their classes by instituting specific rules and procedures (Han et al., 2023).

BOX 3.3: CASE STUDY—MINDESK

The founder/s: Mindesk was co-founded in 2015 by Gabriele Sorrento, who assumed the CEO role, Sergio Giorgio as CTO, and Vittorio Bava as Business Developer. The team brought together a diverse set of skills, with Gabriele's background in engineering and architectural design forming the foundation of the company's business case. Sergio and Vittorio contributed their respective domain experiences. In 2020, the company was acquired, and Mindesk is now part of Vection Technologies' Integrated XR solutions.

Mission and vision: Mindesk's mission is to enhance the efficiency of designers and engineers, mainly dealing with complex assemblies. The team envisioned transitioning CAD software design reviews from printed paper to VR. Today, Mindesk enables teams of different professionals to collaborate in a shared 3D immersive space, which fosters a better understanding of projects, facilitates more insightful contributions, and ultimately leads to faster project approvals.

Case study: Francesco Struglia is an industrial designer at Azimut, specializing in the design of luxury yachts. His boats are known for their organic shapes and meticulous attention to detail. Previously, Francesco would spend days reviewing his CAD drafts before submitting them for production. However, with Mindesk, he can now visualize his CAD designs in 3D, allowing him to see how the boat will look once built. Visualizing the boat on a 1:1 scale gives him greater confidence in the overall correctness of the proportions and ensures that every construction detail is well-designed.

3.2.4 Virtual Reality Headsets

Thanks to VR headsets, users can employ 360° viewing technologies to fully immerse themselves in a three-dimensional (3D) virtual world. The sensors in these viewers track the user's head motions and send that information to the computer, which modifies the virtual environment to reflect the user's movements. Users can explore and engage with the virtual environment in the same way as if they were there in person.

VR viewers are utilized in various industries, including gaming, entertainment, design and engineering, medicine, and scientific study.

Wearable virtual reality headsets let users fully immerse themselves in a three-dimensional (3D) virtual world through 360° viewing technologies. They have eye-covering displays, head-tracking sensors, and user-interactive controllers so that users may engage with the virtual environment.

There are various kinds of virtual reality viewers, including those that use a smartphone or a cable to connect to a computer or gaming console and standalone models that do not need any other equipment to function.

The most potent virtual reality headsets link to a computer or gaming system, but for them to work correctly, they need a strong computer or gaming system. Smartphone-based headsets are less expensive and simpler to use than headsets that link to a computer or gaming console, but they provide a less immersive virtual reality experience. The simplest headsets, like Oculus Quest 2, Pro, or the new Apple Vision Pro, are standalone because they do not need other equipment. They provide a less immersive virtual reality experience than visors with lower-quality graphics connected to a computer or gaming console.

Oculus Quest, HTC Vive, PlayStation VR, Google Cardboard, and the Apple Vision Pro are some of the most well-liked virtual reality viewers. These visors cater to a distinct demographic with unique features and functionality. Oculus Rift, for instance, is one of the most widely used virtual reality gaming viewers, while HTC Vive is frequently used for leisure and business training. Google Cardboard is a low-cost smartphone-based viewer, whereas PlayStation VR is intended for use with the PlayStation gaming system.

VR viewers are used for a variety of purposes. Here are some of the most important ones:

1. *Gaming*: many virtual reality viewers are explicitly made for gaming, providing an immersive playing experience.
2. *Entertainment*: you can use virtual reality viewers to watch movies and videos realistically as if users were truly there when the action was happening.
3. *Education and training*: VR viewers can be used to design immersive and interactive learning experiences, including virtual museum tours or simulations of real-world scenarios.
4. *Design and engineering*: by using virtual reality viewers, 3D models and visualizations may be made more quickly and interactively.
5. Virtual reality headsets can be used to rehabilitate and treat various illnesses, such as phobias or chronic pain, in medicine and scientific

research. Additionally, they can be utilized in academic studies of human behavior under controlled conditions.

BOX 3.4: CASE STUDY—VEESO

The founders: Elia D'Anna and Joseph D'Anna, the dynamic duo behind Veeso, have always been fueled by their unwavering passion for groundbreaking technology and immersive storytelling. From a young age, they were drawn to the limitless possibilities of cutting-edge advancements. After successfully developing web applications within the realms of interactive entertainment and social communication, their attention shifted to the emerging field of virtual reality in 2015. Recognizing the immense potential of VR as a medium, Elia and Joseph became acutely aware of some of its limitations, particularly in face-to-face communication and feelings of isolation. This realization catalyzes the birth of Veeso—an innovative system that revolutionizes how we interact and engage with one another in digital spaces.

Mission and vision: Veeso aims to revolutionize online learning by addressing its limitations and barriers. The company envisions creating an immersive B2B consumer product that ensures the legitimacy and longevity of online education while fostering engagement and interaction among students, educators, and professionals globally.

By leveraging advanced VR facial-tracking technology, Veeso seeks to overcome the lack of face-to-face communication and provide a lifelike digital environment. Their solution eliminates isolation, promotes real-time feedback, and enhances the learning experience, empowering educational institutions, businesses, and professionals in the online learning industry.

Veeso's mission is to transform online learning into a dynamic and interactive experience, bridging the gap between physical and virtual classrooms. With a commitment to innovation and improving educational outcomes, Veeso aims to shape the future of online education, ensuring its effectiveness and credibility in an interconnected world.

Case study: pioneering VR face tracking for the future of communication

Veeso, a VR technology company, emerged in 2016 as a frontrunner in the industry by developing a groundbreaking solution for full-face tracking in VR headsets.

Veeso presents a first-of-its-kind integration of tracking cameras and sensors embedded within the VR headset. This pioneering system can capture the user's facial expressions and emotions in real time, without any training, and seamlessly transfer them into the digital realm. This breakthrough innovation eliminates the barriers of impersonal communication, allowing users to fully express themselves and experience genuine human connections within the virtual environment.

Veeso's Kickstarter campaign attracted widespread attention and support from the growing VR market. With millions of views on news platforms, the campaign showcased the potential of Veeso's VR facial-tracking technology to create immersive social experiences.

By leveraging cameras and sensors, Veeso provided users with accurate and expressive full-face-tracking capabilities. This set them apart from their competitors and positioned them as pioneers in the VR industry.

Veeso's success inspired significant tech companies like Apple and Meta (formerly Facebook) to develop similar technologies. Their early entry into the market showcased the viability and desirability of facial-tracking technology, driving further innovation.

References

Ball, M. (2022). *Metaverso: Cosa Significa, Chi Lo controllerà, e perché sta rivoluzionando le Nostre Vite.* Milano: Garzanti.

Ferrari, P., & Adonopoulos, G. (2021). *NFT: Cosa sono, come funzionano e come investire.* [online] Money. It. Available at: https://www.money.it/NFT-cosa-sono-come-funzionano-come-investire.

Han, E. et al. (2023). People, places, and time: A large-scale, longitudinal study of transformed avatars and environmental context in group interaction in the metaverse. *Journal of Computer-Mediated Communication, 28* (2). doi:10.1093/jcmc/zmac031.

IBM. (2021). *Cos'è la tecnologia blockchain? – IBM Blockchain | IBM.* [online] Available at: https://www.ibm.com/it-it/topics/what-is-blockchain.

Meta. (2021). *Founder's letter, 2021 | Meta.* [online] Available at: https://about.fb.com/news/2021/10/founders-letter/.

Chapter 4

How Technology Is Changing Our Lives

Suppose today we want to take an innovative and technological approach to what is happening to our habits. In that case, we cannot ignore how new specialized tools are changing our social, economic, and relational situations.

If we take a step back and compare today's world with the pre-industrial era of the 1800s, we can better understand the progressive change in our habits and, in a way, a detachment from the real world.

Man in the 1800s was part of the social, economic, and productive context, knowing the dynamics also related to the sense of survival. Man was also a participant and able to deal with issues related to breeding, agriculture, and craftsmanship; elements were helpful and lived to ensure life. In this context, he had developed skills purely associated with observing the reality around him to ensure his and his family's survival in a challenging context.

As also described by Hume, man starts with a disadvantaged state of nature, anthropologically weak, with the sole purpose of satisfying his own selfish needs considering the scarcity of goods, and finds in the artifice of institutions the possibility to survive (Hume, 1982).

This detachment between man and the surrounding reality had its advent in the industrial era, leaving more and more of the rural truth to get closer to the city, to the industrial process, and then technological. The first steps were the advent of the first radio and then television; all this led to the change of social and relational habits, helping to transform the relationships between men, influencing not only ideas, tastes, and orientations but also decisions.

DOI: 10.4324/9781003439691-5

A phenomenon that we can define as social and political has led to the discussion of information of any kind within the reach of everyone, thanks to a simple click.

After television, the next step was interactive virtual reality: it was born from a need not only to make everyone protagonists but also to interpenetrate and interact with the television reality, apparently better than everyday reality.

So, we are at present living during the digital revolution, and as our grandparents tell us or have told us about the changes during the years they lived, so will we with our children and grandchildren.

Something was first introduced with the book *Ready Player One* by Ernest Cline, which then led to the release of the movie *Ready Player One*. The film is set in a worn-out outside world where people, thanks to a new role-playing game, find themselves within a new virtual reality that allows them to reinvent themselves into new characters and be and do what they want. Of course, the plot is very much related to what we are heading toward today, but the ending will have a surprise effect, the rediscovery of the self and the natural and external world, a hybrid world (Cline, 2011).

The advent of the metaverse is upon us. Think of Meta, Roblox, Epic Games, or other digital giants like Tencent. We are familiar with companies that have already announced their launch in the metaverse (Monaco, 2021).

The metaverse is the next bet that combines technology and social media, that is, to create a new virtual world as an evolution of the internet to have access to a new universe of experiences, movies, concerts, meetings, games, and more. Everything imagined or thought of could be achievable virtually. But it will take years before we see the metaverse completed.

What is certain, however, is that the advent of virtual reality has had significant consequences, especially regarding the health of people and young people.

First, the degree of immersive virtual reality suggests an increasing occurrence of subjects who tend to "lock themselves" within a virtual world rather than an actual one, leading to a growing increase in alienation.

Just as is already happening with 2D games, 3D will undoubtedly have more remarkable and influential effects on people's lives.

The real dilemma at first glance is that the virtual world might be more advantageous than the real one. The interaction with other users does not occur directly but through different names and avatars that represent us, so an image of us that, in some ways, could be advantageous in the short term. If we wanted to make parallelism, we could say that in his book *Treatise on*

Human Nature, Hume wrote a thought far from the reality we discussed earlier. A condition where man's interests are directed toward short-term well-being rather than long-term profit: Man is more in favor of what is near to him than of what is farther away (Hume, 1982).

The danger in these cases could be the development of a real community of virtual reality users, which makes us think of the birth of a new form of "social community" and, simultaneously, of individuals disconnected from the surrounding reality but connected to an illusory reality. A thin line that separates us from the perceptual boundary between fact and fiction, which confuses and deludes the mind through strange sensations, creating new illusory beliefs that could lead us to think of new habits, where virtual reality can be better in many ways.

Another aspect that should not be underestimated is the lack of perception of one's body weight, of pain, also distorting the perception of our abilities, up to the worst-case that leads to desensitization and loss of reception of external stimuli.

So, reflecting well on the type of dissociation these tools involve, the consequences, not only on society but especially on the individual, can be different and should not be taken lightly.

Of course, reading these last lines, which I admit can be uncomfortable, a reflection immediately arises: Is there a way to use these new tools in an advantageous manner that can positively impact humans?

References

Cline, E. (2011). *Player one*. Milano: Isbn Edizioni.

Hume, D. (1982). *Trattato sulla natura umana*. Bari: Laterza.

Monaco, D. (2021). *Da Microsoft a Tencent: Tutte le aziende che stanno investendo nel metaverso*. [online] Wired Italia. Available at: https://www.wired.it/article/metaverso-microsoft-tencent-cina-facebook/.

Chapter 5

Virtual Reality and Augmented Reality

5.1 Studies and Research

We cannot ignore the advent of VR, AR, and AI, which will be part of the metaverse. They could help increase the quality of work and create new ways to train people without time and space constraints.

Studies conducted in VR began in the 1980s; one of the first tests was handled by flight simulator training in Ohio between the 1960s and 1970s (McLellan, 1996). According to Chen (2006), it could be used as a support so that training can improve understanding of performance. The model, created in 1999, realized that VR and its use could facilitate learning complex subjects and abstract concepts (Salzman et al., 1999). Physics students performed a useful and helpful experiment for understanding the qualitative dimensions of phenomena, and the results were completely different (Cheen, 2001). How is it possible to study, view, and understand an abstract and complex subject that is changing? Moreover, the implications of this phenomenon will increase the quality of scientific research. However, the importance of using VR in education and training has advantages and disadvantages.

Starting with the advantages regarding the sense of presence, students can understand more complex topics while having fun and interacting with the environment. VR can generate constructivism theory where educational applications can be developed. Last but not least, in a virtual world, it is

DOI: 10.4324/9781003439691-6

possible to manipulate objects, and, according to Pantalidis, this technology can provide a new sense of visualization by reproducing an alternative method of presenting materials (Pandalidis, 2009).

To give an accurate and precise description, within Elviesan's article, we find:

> VR can be defined as "the total of hardware and software systems that seek to perfect an all-encompassing sensory illusion of being present in another environment." Immersion, presence, and interactivity are considered the fundamental characteristics of VR technologies. The term interactivity can be described as the degree to which a user can modify the VR environment in real time. Presence is "the subjective experience of being in one place or environment, even when physically located in another" (Witmer & Singer, 1998). While researchers largely agree on the definitions of interactivity and presence, there are differing opinions on immersion. One branch of researchers suggests that immersion should be viewed as a technological attribute that can be objectively assessed (Slater & Wilbur, 1997), while others describe immersion as a subjective and individual belief, i.e., a psychological phenomenon (Witmer & Singer, 1998). Jensen and Konradsen (2018) suggest an additional perspective regarding the positive effects of immersion and attendance on learning outcomes. The results of the studies reviewed in their paper show that students who used an immersive HMD were more engaged, spent more time on learning tasks, and acquired better cognitive, psychomotor, and affective skills. However, this study also identifies many factors that may be reinforcers or barriers to immersion and presence. The graphical quality of VR and awareness when using VR, for example, may reduce the sense of presence. Individual personality traits may also be associated with limited skill acquisition from VR technologies.

On the other hand, the cost and time to learn how to use the software and hardware are high. Likewise, it will not be used as a replacement for trainers and teachers, and interaction with real humans is required. In addition, the inaccurate use of VR could harm physically and emotionally.

Due to Tractica's research on VR, the VR hardware and software market will grow from $1 billion in 2018 to $12.6 billion in 2025. The effect includes several sectors: marketing, finance, human resources, and manufacturing.

In addition, VR will also impact customers. Products can be presented as a showcase, and marketing will be different. Thanks to this system, a considerable amount of data will be available on how people act and interact. For example, it will be possible to try out a new car or furniture, or kitchenware, as Ikea is doing using virtual showrooms.

5.2 Augmented Reality

The term was attributed to Boing researcher Tom Caudell in 1990 (Lee, 2012). AR is spreading, especially in education, advertising, maintenance, and marketing and is helping companies train employees to work faster and more effectively. In addition, other advantages of three-dimensional models include the use of images, text, videos, and experiences and the ability to visualize the final product on the table. About 70% of accidents are caused by human error since operators do not know how to proceed. Thanks to these technologies, there is the possibility to increase the quality of performance and tasks up to 50% faster than the traditional way, reducing the percentage of errors and risks. Think about the mere fact that people can simulate something before you do it. AR has emerged in recent years; the areas of success are education, entertainment, advertising, and medicine. Some applications in industries for maintenance are aimed at speeding up learning and performing operations. In addition, professional authoring is programming and modeling new projects to create children's books in AR (Ramirez et al., 2013).

As we can understand, the advantages of VR and AR are cost reduction and the possibility to minimize risks. With VR, we can also find several limitations; for example, when people train in a virtual environment, it is still determined that the same will happen in the natural environment, where preparation is the only way to prevent the future or avoid serious failures.

More than 30 years ago, VR and AR were only used in the military and gaming; due to cost, it was impossible to introduce them in the commercial world.

Several projects are conducted with VR, an example of an application can be seen in Israel; the city 5,000 years ago was reconstructed, and people could visit them in a virtual environment.

There are many differences between VR and AR. AR is less mature due to technological limitations, lack of standardization, and higher prices.

5.3 What It Is and How It Works

With headsets like VR viewers, VR gloves, and motion controllers, VR allows users to interact with a simulated 3D environment in a completely realistic way. Numerous uses for VR exist, including gaming, learning, designing, and therapy.

VR headsets like the Oculus Quest 2, 3 and Pro, HTC Vive, and Pico VR are used to access VR and provide an immersive experience. High-resolution displays and motion sensors are included in VR viewers, allowing users to see and engage with the simulated environment.

Applications for VR include gaming, education, design, and treatment, among many more. VR in gaming enables players to become fully immersed in simulated environments, communicate with virtual characters, and participate in immersive adventures. VR can be used in education and training to develop immersive learning environments and simulations that let students explore and engage with abstract ideas. Moreover, it helps us in project planning and product design, allowing consumers to explore a space before it is built visually. VR is also used in therapeutic settings to treat phobias and chronic pain.

5.4 How to Create Content

Creating VR content requires specific techniques and tools, such as 3D modeling and motion capture. 3D modeling allows businesses to create three-dimensional models of objects and environments that can be used within a VR experience. On the other hand, motion capture allows human body movements to be recorded and used to animate virtual characters within a VR experience.

Several platforms and game engines, including Unity and Unreal Engine, are available for VR content creation. Unity is a cross-platform development platform that allows developers to create VR content. Unreal Engine is a game engine used to create high-performance VR games and applications. Both game engines offer various tools and features for creating VR content, including 3D modeling, animation, lighting, and physics.

BOX 5.1: CASE STUDY—GRAVITY SKETCH ON META QUEST STORE

Gravity Sketch is a 3D design and collaboration tool that enables users to create vehicles, sneakers, furniture, characters, art, and more; express their ideas with 3D strokes and geometry; solve complex design challenges working directly in 3D at any scale, all with a fun and intuitive toolset that makes working in 3D easy; and collaborate with others by jumping into the same virtual studio to share their ideas, hold a design review, or co-create together from anywhere in the world.

Other tools and technologies used to create VR content include spatial audio, which enables the creation of an immersive audio experience, and motion detection, which enables the creation of interactive experiences.

Creating content for VR requires using specific techniques and tools, such as 3D modeling and motion capture, and using platforms and game engines, such as Unity and Unreal Engine. There are also different technologies to create an immersive experience, such as spatial audio and motion detection. A VR project requires an extensive and specialized work team.

5.5 Interactions

One of the main features of VR is the ability to interact with the simulated environment naturally and intuitively. There are several ways to interact with VR content, including using motion controllers and VR gloves. Motion controllers, such as Oculus Touch or HTC Vive Controller, allow users to explore and interact with the simulated environment using hand movements. These controllers often include motion sensors and buttons for interaction. VR gloves, such as Manus VR, allow users to interface with the simulated environment more precisely and naturally. VR gloves can include motion sensors and buttons for interaction, and pressure and force sensors to make the experience more immersive.

In addition, voice and facial recognition can interact with VR content. For example, voice can be used to issue commands to virtual characters and the system, while facial recognition can make the interaction more natural and personalized.

Several modes of interaction with VR content include motion controllers, VR gloves, voice commands, and facial recognition. These interaction modes allow users to explore and interact with the simulated environment naturally and intuitively, making the experience more immersive.

5.6 Why Use VR

VR can be used for various applications, including gaming, training, design, and therapy.

In gaming, VR allows users to immerse themselves in simulated worlds and interact with virtual characters. Numerous VR games are available on different platforms, including PCs, game consoles, and mobile devices. For example, there are VR games such as Beat Saber, which allows users to use motion controllers to cut down blocks flying toward them, or Half-Life: Alyx, a first-person action game in a fully immersive environment.

In education and training, virtual reality can create immersive learning environments and simulations that allow students to explore and interact with abstract concepts. For example, virtual reality can be used to create a learning environment for surgery, where students can practice surgical techniques in a safe and controlled manner.

Virtual reality can be used professionally for product design and project planning. For example, architects can use virtual reality to create models of buildings and visualize how they will look when built. In contrast, companies can use virtual reality to create training environments and accident simulations to prepare their employees for emergencies.

VR is also used to treat disorders such as phobia and chronic pain in therapeutic settings. VR can be used for gradual exposure to phobias, such as fear of flying or insects. Distinguishing between real and false will become increasingly complex. How can people make informed decisions when the boundaries between real and false are severely blurred? (Carciofi, 2022).

5.7 The Future

VR is an ever-evolving technology, and several emerging trends mark the future of VR.

One of the most important trends is increased image quality and performance.

The adoption of VR is increasing in various fields, such as education, training, and work, and this trend is expected to continue to expand in the future. VR is also increasingly used in medicine, architecture, and the automotive industry. AR and mixed reality (MR) are other emerging technologies that are being developed and could affect the future of VR. AR allows users to view virtual elements superimposed on reality, while MR combines virtual and AR elements to create a hybrid experience. These technologies are expected to be combined with VR to create even more immersive and interactive experiences. In addition, there are concerns about the social and ethical implications of the expansion of VR, such as the effect on social communication and human interaction and the need to establish guidelines and standards to ensure the safety of users.

The future of VR is promising with several emerging trends, such as increased image quality and performance, adoption in different domains, and the emergence of new technologies such as AR and MR.

BOX 5.2: CASE STUDY—VHIL STANFORD LAB

If you are in California, you cannot miss the VHIL, or the Virtual Human Interaction Lab at Stanford. Founded in 2003, the lab aims to understand better the psychological and behavioral effects of VR and AR. Researchers are trying to answer the focus and questions: what psychological processes operate when people use VR and AR? How does this medium fundamentally transform people and society? What happens when anyone can have a perfect experience at the touch of a button? Moreover, how can we actively seek to create and consume VR that enhances instead of detracts from the real world? (VHIL, Stanford).

References

Carciofi, A. (2022). *Vivere IL metaverso: Vita, Lavoro E relazioni: Come trovare benessere Ed Equilibrio nel futuro di internet.* Macerata: ROI.

Chee, Y. (2001). Virtual reality in education: Rooting learning in experience. In *Proceedings of the international symposium on virtual education 2001, Busan, South Korea* (pp. 43–54). Busan, Korea: Symposium Organizing Committee, Dongseo University. Available at: http://yamsanchee.myplace.nie.edu.sg/Publications/2001/ISVE2001 Invited.pdf.

Chen, C. (2006). *The design, development, and evaluation of a virtual reality-based learning environment* (pp. 39–63). [ebook] Australasian Journal of Educational Technology.

Jensen, L., & Konradsen, F. (2018). A review of the use of virtual reality head-mounted displays in education and training. *Education and Information Technologies*, 23(4), 1515–1529. http://doi.org/10.1007/s10639-017-9676-0.

Lee, K. (2012). Augmented reality in education and training. *TechTrends*, 56(2), pp. 13–21. http://doi.org/10.1007/s11528-012-0559-3.

McLellan, H. (1996). *Virtual realities* (pp. 461–497). [ebook] Available at: http://citeseerx.ist.psu.edu/viewdoc/download?doi=10.1.1.108.3221&rep=rep1&type=pdf.

Pantelidis, V. (2009). *Reasons to use virtual reality in education and training courses and a model to determine when to use virtual reality* (pp. 59–70). [ebook] Klidarithmos Computer Books. Available at: https://files.eric.ed.gov/fulltext/EJ1131313.pdf.

Ramirez, H., Gonzalez Mendivil, E., Flores, P., & Gonzalez, M. (2013). *Authoring software for augmented reality applications for maintenance and training processes*. [ebook] Elsevier. Available at: https://pdf.sciencedirectassets.com/.

Salzman, M.C., Dede, C., Loftin, R.B., & Chen, J. (1999). A model for understanding how virtual reality aids complex conceptual learning. *Presence: Teleoperators and Virtual Environments*, 8, 293–316.

Slater, M., & Wilbur, S. (1997). A framework for immersive virtual environments (five): Speculations on the role of presence in virtual environments. *Presence: Teleoperators and Virtual Environments*, 6(6), 603–616. http://doi.org/10.1162/pres.1997.6.6.603.

VHIL. Available at: https://stanfordvr.com/.

Witmer, B.G., & Singer, M.J. (1998). Measuring presence in virtual environments: A presence questionnaire. *Presence: Teleoperators and Virtual Environments*, 7, 225–240. http://doi.org/10.1162/105474698565686.

Chapter 6

A Super Artificial Worker

AI is a modern discipline that has recently contributed to the progress of the entire computer system. AI is influenced by many fields, starting from philosophy, mathematics, economics, neuroscience, psychology, cybernetics, cognitive science, and linguistics.

According to the proven and internationally accepted definition,

> AI belongs to computer science, which studies the theoretical foundations, methodologies, and techniques that enable the design of hardware and software systems that can simulate human performance. In addition, AI is an experimental discipline, and the system is only able to meet objectives if they are measurable.

The aim of the discipline is not to replicate or simulate human intelligence, which for several experts is impossible to do for epistemological reasons, but to affect human intelligence; in fact, there is no a priori reason why some performances of human intelligence, for example, the ability to solve problems thanks to inferential procedures, can be provided by a machine. Taking into account the process of "emulation," the performance of intelligence is obtained using specific machine mechanisms, which are different from the human one but can be qualitatively equivalent and quantitatively superior to the human one (in the following chapters, we will analyze several case studies). Thanks to the results and studies conducted, experts have evaluated several anthropomorphic type models, which allow not only to obtain human-like performance but also to adopt methods used by humans and not to ensure the best possible results. The latter model has shown great adaptation and integration.

DOI: 10.4324/9781003439691-7

According to Nilsson, AI is both science and engineering. It is a science because we can get experimental and scientific confirmation when certain intelligent behaviors are emulated with synthetic systems. In addition, AI is also engineering because performance is achieved by machines that imitate certain behaviors, erroneously considered inaccessible to the artificial world; this is a concrete contribution to improving human life.

6.1 The Rise of AI

The first computers could only make calculations and manipulate symbols, features taken from human abilities. AI's official date of birth is 1956, during the famous summer seminar at Dartmouth College in Hanover, where several scientists participated in the workshop setting a new goal: machines would be able to think with the efficiency of humans within a few years.

When we talk about the history of AI, we start in 1956. Still, we have to refer to cybernetics and the first electronic computers, starting from Charles Babbage with the analytical engine, Gottfried Wilhelm Leibniz with the mechanized reason, Ramon Llull with the logic engine, and the self-propelled automata of Heron of Alexandria. However, to solve the problem related to AI, we use the date 1956 because of the computer science research of the foundation of AI that had begun in the 1950s.

In this historical context, it is relevant to mention McCorduck. Following the formalistic tradition of investigating the mind, several ideas have emerged: artificial performance is a part of human practice as natural performance in its continuous work to imitate and reproduce itself and nature. The historical framework of the discipline, which in the case of AI appears problematic, is a critical point to start from and opens up questions regarding the determination of its particular ontological status.

Within the summer workshop at Dartmouth College, we can also find Marvin Minsky, a junior follower of math and neurology at Harvard, Nathaniel Rochester, research director at IBM, and Claude Elwood Shannon, a well-known mathematician. The main subject of the workshop was "brainstorming," opening a discussion on how to reproduce partial intelligence with an electronic computer through a new theoretical approach. The years following the Dartmouth workshop were characterized by high expectations, also based on the success of computer systems.

The decline of this period of neural networks resulted from the criticism received by Minky on the "perceptron," a theory of Frank Rosenblatt that could not recognize visual stimuli.

An interesting case study was the AI victory in the game of chess, checkers, and sighting realized by McCarthy. The enthusiasm for these early results was based on general mechanisms and limiting notions of AI.

Only now we can develop machines that can conduct mathematical and logical reasoning like humans, even if they must master at least seven types of intelligence (see Table 7.1 in Chapter 7) before their intelligence can be compared to ours. The problem proposed at Dartmouth College was in the hardware, the ability to do computations with sufficient speed. In addition, the challenge, which also turns out to be a current problem, is that we need to understand human reasoning, leading to problems in simulations. If we consider the Wright brothers, they were successful not because they simulated birds but because they understood the processes used by birds and went deeper into aerodynamics studies (Massaron & Mueller, 2020).

6.2 The Resurgence of AI

The term "AI winter," meaning the AI crisis, refers to a period when researchers see reduced investment in research and development. This happens when results do not meet excessive expectations.

Right now, AI is in a good phase, thanks to "machine learning" (ML), a technology that can help computers learn data. However, ML translation has several criticisms. For example, it can perform a task incorrectly, especially when input is incorrect.

Nowadays, the best solution is based on "deep learning" (DL), which aims to replicate all parts of our brain. At the moment, DL can be supported by powerful computers, sophisticated algorithms, and big data sets, thanks to significant investments from companies like Google, Facebook, and Amazon that are increasing research for their interests.

6.3 Strong and Weak AI

There are two types of AI: strong and weak.

Strong AI:

Strong artificial intelligence (AI), also known as artificial general intelligence (AIG) or general AI, is a theoretical form of AI used to describe a certain mindset of AI development. If researchers can develop strong AI, the machine would require an intelligence equal to human intelligence; it would have a self-aware consciousness that can solve problems, learn, and plan for the future.

(IBM, 2020)

To understand strong AI, we need to analyze the necessary tests: the Turing Test and the Chinese Room Argument (CRA).

On the other hand, weak AI:

Weak artificial intelligence (AI)—also called restricted AI—is a type of artificial intelligence limited to a specific area. It simulates human cognition. It can benefit society by automating time-consuming tasks and analyzing data in ways humans cannot. Weak AI can be contrasted with strong AI.

Weak AI lacks human consciousness, and the classic illustration of weak AI is John Searle's Chinese room.

6.4 The Chinese Room

In 1980, John Searle, in the article "Mind, Brains, and Programs," published in "Behavioral and Brain Sciences," tried to refute the Turing Test, according to which a computer can deceive a human. The article's hypothesis is based on functionalism, which is the ability to simulate specific characteristics of the human mind (Searle, 1980).

The Chinese room is based on two tests. In the first test, someone creates an AI that can understand Chinese characters and uses a set of rules to create an answer; it returns the output from these characters. The AI gives the correct answer, and those outside the room cannot tell if it is human or AI. The second test seeks to demonstrate the ability to use formal rules to get an output (syntax), which differs from understanding what it is doing (semantics).

The central theme reflects whether AI can understand what it is doing (artificial solid intelligence) versus weak AI, which follows the rules for specific problems (Massaron & Mueller, 2020).

Today, all available AI is weak: it cannot understand what it is doing.

Referring to the movie *Ex Machina*, again starting from a dialogue between Nathan and Cheb, at about 1 hour and 25 minutes into the movie, the machine was given the task to escape and had to use: self-awareness, imagination, manipulation, sensuality, and empathy.

6.5 The Four AI

In the previous paragraphs, we analyzed the difference between strong and weak AI with the help of the Chinese room experiment.

Arend Hintze, researcher and professor of AI, proposed a different classification of AI, dividing it into four types:

Type 1: Reactive Machines

An example of reactive machines is those that defeat humans in chess; Deep Blue, IBM's chess-playing supercomputer, beat international grandmaster Garry Kasparov in the late 1990s. The reactive machine has no memory or experience and bases its decisions on its ability to process intelligent algorithms. Beyond that, there is Google's AlphaGo, which has beaten the best human Go experts. Its analysis is more sophisticated than Deep Blue's since it uses a neural network.

Type 2: Limited Memory

Self-driving cars and independent robots can only take time in some decisions to choose the right one. They have a small amount of memory to store the knowledge and experience needed to handle different situations.

Type 3: Theory of Mind

At this point, the author distinguishes between our machines and the machines we will build. In future stages, machines can form representations about the world and other agents or entities. In psychology, this is called the "theory of mind."

A self-driving car needs this type of AI. This means that a self-driving car must be able to get from one point to another, pick up on the intentions of other drivers who may be in conflict, and react accordingly.

Type 4: Self-Awareness

This type of AI can only be seen in movies because it requires technologies that do not exist today. This system can form a representation of itself that is an extension of the "theory of mind." Consciousness is called "self-awareness": for whatever reason, I can say, "I want that object," but it is a different statement than "I know I want that object." Conscious beings are self-aware of internal states and can predict the feelings of others (Hintze, 2016).

Intelligence is not artificial; humans and researchers try to build intelligence inspired by human intelligence.

6.6 Advantages and Disadvantages of Learning with AI

Using AI in learning can offer many advantages and present some challenges. Here are some of the main advantages and disadvantages of using AI in learning:

- *Personalization of learning*: AI can personalize learning according to a student's needs, such as providing lessons on specific topics based on the student's previous performance or learning preferences.
- *Personalized feedback*: AI can provide personalized feedback to students on their progress, such as providing suggestions for improvement or emphasizing students' areas of strength.
- *Performance assessment*: AI can assess student performance by analyzing students' responses to assignments or open-ended questions.
- *Teaching support*: AI can support teachers in preparing lessons, for example, by providing personalized teaching materials.

It also presents significant disadvantages and challenges that cannot be overlooked:

- *Dependence on technology*: the use of AI in learning depends on the availability of technology, such as computers or mobile devices, which can be challenging for some students.
- *Lack of human interaction*: AI can only partially replace human interaction in learning, and some students may miss the presence of a teacher or interaction with classmates.
- *Risk of bias*: AI is only as good as the data it uses to learn, so there is a risk that it may replicate biases in the data.
- *Security risks*: AI depends on access to data so that student data can be compromised or AI is used for malicious purposes.
- *Costs*: AI may require the purchase of specific hardware and software, which can cost schools or colleges.

AI can be a helpful tool to support learning, but it is essential to consider the possible drawbacks and take appropriate steps to address them.

6.7 AI Chase and Golden Years?

AI is a rapidly developing field that has made many advances in recent decades. Many notable successes have been in using AI to solve complex problems, such as word and image recognition, machine translation, autonomous driving, and data analysis. However, much work still needs to be done to develop AI to address a broader range of problems and become truly "intelligent" like humans. In addition, AI also presents ethical and social challenges that need to be addressed to ensure its responsible and sustainable use. So while we can certainly say that 2022 and 2023 are periods of significant progress in AI, we cannot say that we are in the "golden years" of AI.

Here are some examples:

Many examples exist on how AI is used today to solve complex problems and automate repetitive tasks. Here are some examples:

- *Word and image recognition*: AI recognizes words and images accurately and quickly. For example, speech recognition apps use AI to convert speech into written text, while image recognition systems can be used to classify and identify objects in photos and videos.
- *Machine translation*: AI automatically translates text from one language to another, enabling people who speak different languages to communicate efficiently.
- *Autonomous driving*: AI is used to develop vehicles that can drive themselves, using sensors and algorithms to interpret the world around them and make decisions about how to move.
- *Data analysis*: AI analyzes large amounts of data and extracts valuable information, such as identifying hidden trends or patterns. For example, AI analyzes financial data to predict market movements or health data to identify disease patterns.

These are just a few examples of how AI is used today. In many other fields, AI is used to solve complex problems and automate repetitive tasks.

BOX 6.1: CASE STUDY—OPENAI LAUNCHED CHATGPT

OpenAI is an AI research and deployment company. Their mission is to ensure that artificial general intelligence benefits all of humanity with the mission of creating artificial general intelligence (AGI) that is smarter than humans for the benefit of all of humanity (OpenAI).

ChatGPT is an interesting case study for different reasons:

■ It has over 100 million users.
■ In 5 days, it got 1 million users.
■ Openai.com has 1 billion views each month.

Here is another statistic to consider.

From Figure 6.1, we can see that ChatGPT has surpassed all the previous records, reaching 100M users in less than one week. The exciting aspect of ChatGPT is that it opens the door to AI, and all big tech is now running to create their generative AI software.

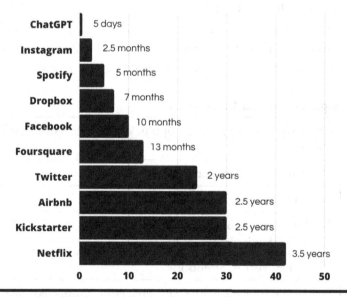

Figure 6.1 ChatGPT. Personal elaboration.

Let us analyze some pros:

■ fast response time
■ human-like response
■ supports more than 20+ languages
■ easy to use

On the other hand, the cons:

■ errors and wrong information
■ bias responses due to the data

ChatGPT is a powerful tool but still needs some improvement and documentation on how to use it properly (Durante, 2023).

6.8 A Super Artificial Worker

Let us look at some projects and categories to watch out for (Table 6.1).

According to Forbes, AI is currently having a "hot topic" moment as programs like ChatGPT demonstrate how strong and capable it is becoming.

In recent months, the introduction of this new breed of "generative" AI tools has demonstrated that the field is no longer limited to academic research or Silicon Valley tech titans.

Moreover, far from being just the newest "viral sensation," AI has developed into a technology that any company or person can use to transform how they conduct business or carry out various daily tasks.

Table 6.1 Example of New AI Companies

Text	ChatGPT, Notion, Jasper, Copy.ai, Writesonic, Frase, Surfer, Outplay, Mem, You
Voice	VoiceAI, Resemble, PlayHt
Audio	Eleven Labs, Murf, Supetone
Coding	GitHub Copilot, BlackBox, Tabnine, Mintlify, Stenografy, Enzyme, Debuild, Seek
Legal	DoNotPay, Ferret, Spellbook
Video	Synthesia, Runway, Luma, Lumen5, Hour One, Fliki, Tavus, Colossyan, Rephrase.ai
Productivity	Productivity Hero, Channel, Heyday
Meeting	Sembly, Attention, Fireflies
Image	Lensa, NightCafe, Craiyon, OpenArt, Mindjourney, Dall-E 2, Poly, Vizcom, Aragon

The job is changing. The way they train and coach people is changing. The relationship between machines and AI is changing. Everything depends on how we implement new technologies that will shape our future.

Generative AI, which involves using AI to process extensive amounts of data and create original content, has a history dating back several decades. One of the earliest examples is the ELIZA chatbot from the 1960s, which allowed users to input questions and receive seemingly unique responses. However, ELIZA's answers were based on a predefined set of rules. A significant breakthrough came in 2014 with Ian Goodfellow's introduction of generative adversarial networks (GANs) at Gojust. GANs involved pitting two networks against each other in a zero-sum game to generate realistic low-resolution images. While the quality of the generated images improved over time, GANs remained challenging to train and scale.

In 2017, another group at Google released the influential "Attention Is All You Need" paper, which introduced the transformers concept. Transformers were designed to enhance the performance of text translation by leveraging attention mechanisms that provide contextual understanding based on word positions. The researchers discovered that models incorporating these attention mechanisms outperformed other methods of extracting patterns from text. Transformers revolutionized training efficiency by allowing parallel processing of entire text strings instead of analyzing word by word. This breakthrough enabled the development of Generative Pretrained Transformers (GPTs), now used in applications such as ChatGPT, GitHub Copilot, and Microsoft's Bing search engine. These models were trained on vast collections of human language and are called Large Language Models (LLMs).

While transformers have proven effective in computer vision tasks, an alternative approach called latent diffusion, also known as stable diffusion, has emerged as a powerful method for generating high-resolution images. Startups like Stability and Midjourney have developed diffusion models that combine the strengths of GANs, transformers, and even physics. Remarkably, these models achieve impressive results while remaining significantly smaller than the latest GPTs. The open-source availability of some of these models has fostered a culture of experimentation and innovation among individuals seeking to explore generative AI (Buhler, 2023b).

Moreover, let us analyze what Sequoia published about the top AI 50 (Buhler, 2023a) (Figure 6.2).

CONSUMER USER		ENTERPRICE STACK			INDUSTRIES VERTICAL					
					LAW FIRMS	CREATIVE	HEALTH	DEFENCE	AGRICULTURE & CLIMATE	CONSTRUCTION
ENTERTAINMENT	character.ai	GENERAL PRODUCTIVITY	ADEPT TOME	GLEAN ALPHASENSE	Harvey.	runway	iz.ai	undurial	Pachama	Canvas
	Mindjourney	GENERAL & ADMINISTRATIVE	IRONCLAD EIGHTFOLD.AI	SYNTHESIA		Mindjourney	Bayesian	Shield AI	FarmWise	
PRODUCTIVITY	OpenAI ChatGPT	SALES & CONSUMER SUPPORT	GONG CLARY	REVCOMM POLYAI		imagen	insitro	SlingShot		
	neeva	MARKETING	JASPER	WRITER		descript	Path.AI	Vannevar Labs		
OTHER	Trigo waabi	EPT/IT/SECURITY	MOVEWORKS VECTRA	ABNORMAL GITHUB			UNLEARN			

DEPLOY & MONITOR	HUGGING FACE	ARIZE		FULL STACK LARGE LANGUAGE MODELS		
TRAIN & FINE TUNE MODELS	WEIGHTS & BIASES MOSAIC	PYTORCH		OpenAI	ANTHROPIC	cohere
USE OPEN SOURCE MODELS & FRAMEWORK	HUGGING FACE	STANFORD APLPACA	LLaMA	character.ai	Inflection	

STORE & COMPUTE					HARDWARE	
LABEL / PROCESS DATA		DATA WAREHOUSE / LAKEHOUSE		CLOUD SERVICE PROVIDER	NVIDIA	AMD
SNORKEJ SCALE SURGE COACTIVE		SNOWFLAKE DATABRICKS		GOOGLE CLOUD AWS AZURE	INTEL	

Figure 6.2   AI 50 2023.

6.8.1 *Generative AI Infrastructure*

OpenAI garnered significant attention last year with the launch of ChatGPT and this year with the introduction of GPT-4. However, they are just some players in the field of LLMs. Anthropic has developed its chatbot Claude, which utilizes Reinforcement Learning Constitutional AI (RL-CAI) to incorporate human-friendly principles and prevent abuse and misinformation in its outputs. Inflection, a secretive startup founded by DeepMind's Mustafa Suleyman and Greylock's Reid Hoffman, is focused on consumer applications.

These high-profile entrants are just a few examples in the closed-source domain. In the realm of open source, Hugging Face has become a popular platform for developers who want to train their models or fine-tune existing ones. Alongside Stability's open-source offerings, Hugging Face hosts state-of-the-art models such as Facebook's LLaMA and Stanford's Alpaca.

6.8.2 *Predictive Infrastructure*

During technological shifts, investors often focus on companies providing novel infrastructure solutions. Given that AI revolves around prediction, this emerging category is called predictive infrastructure. The most prominent players in this field host vast data for enterprise AI applications, facilitating data pipelines. Databricks, for instance, has differentiated itself from established companies like Snowflake.

Since processes like data labeling and cleaning are crucial for model training, there are now four companies in this category on this year's list: Coactive, Scale, Snorkel, and Surge. Two newcomers, MosaicML and Weights & Biases, specialize in assisting AI practitioners with training and fine-tuning models. Arize and Hugging Face make it easier to deploy models at scale.

6.8.3 Generative AI Applications

Midjourney and stable diffusion gained popularity on social media, bringing generative AI to the forefront of popular culture. ChatGPT then captured global attention, becoming the fastest product to reach 100 million users. While Google introduced its Bard chatbot in response, Neeva became the first generative AI-native search engine.

As LLMs were primarily designed for generating text, the category of generative writing apps has experienced rapid growth. Two examples on this year's list are Jasper, which utilizes GPT-4 to assist marketing copywriters, and writer, which has trained its proprietary model for enterprise use cases. Language models' increased capabilities now extend to more complex applications, including legal text. Harvey employs GPT-4 for associate-level legal work at law firms and professional services companies, while Ironclad automates various contract processes for in-house legal teams.

Generative AI's inherent creativity has also sparked innovation in other creative fields. Runway generates, edits, and applies video effects that meet the quality standards of the Oscar-winning team behind "Everything Everywhere All at Once." Descript streamlines podcast and video workflows by leveraging generative AI to simplify editing. While ChatGPT, Bing, and Bard serve as general-purpose chatbots, there is a nascent creative space for crafting custom chatbots powered by Character AI, founded by one of the authors of the original Transformer paper Noam Shazeer.

For many individuals, creating PowerPoint presentation represents their creative outlet at work. New generative AI apps like Tome make it effortless to design visually appealing presentations that bring ideas to life using only text prompts. Adept offers a different approach to work productivity by building an action model, ACT-1, trained on how people interact with their computers. The goal is to eventually automate specific tasks, reducing the need for manual searching, clicking, and scrolling.

6.8.4 Predictive AI Applications

Another valuable use of AI's predictive power is detecting anomalies and finding ways to mitigate them. Abnormal Security, for example, analyzes a company's cloud email environment to identify phishing attempts and other threats, removing malicious emails. In the medical field, Viz.ai rapidly identifies patient imaging that requires specialist review and coordinates the care team to enhance outcomes for time-sensitive conditions like stroke.

References

Buhler, K. (2023a). *AI 50 2023*. Sequoia Capital US/Europe. Available at: https://www.sequoiacap.com/article/ai-50-2023/.

Buhler, K. (2023b). *Generative AI is exploding. These are the most important trends you need to know*. Forbes. Available at: https://www.forbes.com/sites/konstantinebuhler/2023/04/11/ai-50-2023-generative-ai-trends/.

Duarte, F. (2023). *Number of CHATGPT users (2023)*. Exploding Topics. Available at: https://explodingtopics.com/blog/chatgpt-users.

Hintze, A. (2016). *Understanding the four types of AI, from reactive robots to self-aware beings*. [online] The conversation. Available at: https://theconversation.com/understanding-the-four-types-of-ai-from- reactive-robots-to-self-aware-beings-67616.

IBM. (2020). *Strong AI*. [online] Available at: https://www.ibm.com/cloud/learn/strong-ai.

Massaron, L., & Mueller, J. (2020). *Intelligenza artificiale for dummies*. Milano: U. Hoepli.

Searle, J.R. (1980). Minds, brains, and programs. *Behavioral and Brain Sciences*, 3(3), 417–424. doi:10.1017/s0140525x00005756.

TECHNICAL AND PHILOSOPHICAL ISSUES

Chapter 7

Artificial and Human Intelligence

The programmer is the creator, while the hardware is the blind executor of the program.

(Federico Faggin)

We need new skills to understand what is going on, but more importantly, to make qualitative and quantitative decisions for our future.

We have always talked about vertical skills, but in a fast-changing world, especially the technological world, more than having technical skills is needed, as is having only business skills. We need a new key, something that not only gives us the ability to develop or grow a business concretely but also has less tangible aspects, such as philosophy but helps us understand what principles to use to build or direct our business.

Let us look at the evolution over time and how things evolve today (Figure 7.1).

At the beginning, when technology had not yet evolved, the skills required by the market were few, and the aspects of success were business-related and managerial skills. As technology evolved and tangible results of how certain hardware and software were becoming more and more valuable, the need for figures with vertical technical skills grew. Today that is no longer enough. The market is changing rapidly, and the skills required are changing, especially the ability and critical thinking, even more so. Being

DOI: 10.4324/9781003439691-9

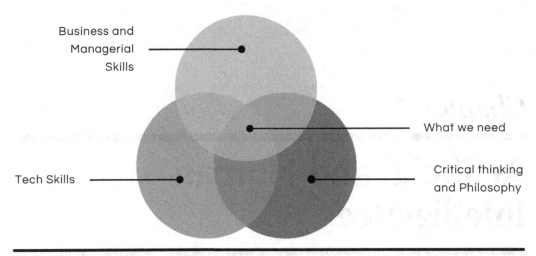

Figure 7.1   Business <> philosophy <> technology. Personal elaboration.

able to produce something is essential, but understanding even more of the why and the consequences of what is being made is of even greater value. Society and companies will increasingly need people who not only know how to create and then have as their goal a particular product but also all the critical aspects that can arise from what is created.

Let us start by analyzing the difference between human and artificial intelligence.

Human intelligence must include a variety of mental activities:

■ *Learning:* the ability to obtain and process new information;
■ *Thinking: the* ability to manipulate information;
■ *Understanding:* considering the results of controlling information;
■ *Grasping the truth:* determining whether the information is valid or not;
■ *Perform relationships:* whether accurate data can interact with other data;
■ *Consider meaning:* apply truth in particular situations that are consistent with their relationships;
■ *Separate facts from beliefs:* determine if data are supported by reliable sources where consistency and validity can be demonstrated.

Humans do not employ only one type of intelligence, but we use different types of intelligence, as seen in Table 7.1.

In Table 7.1, by analyzing the seven types of intelligence, we can understand what our brain can do and what a machine can simulate. Now let us take a closer look at each one.

Table 7.1 Understanding Types of Intelligence

Types	Potential of Simulation	Human Tools
Visual-spatial	Moderate	Models, charts, diagrams, photographs, drawings, 3D modeling, video, television, and multimedia
Body-kinesthetic	Moderate to high	Specialized devices and natural objects
Creative	None	Artistic productions, new thought patterns, inventions, and new types of musical composition
Interpersonal	Poor to moderate	Telephone, audio, video teleconferencing, writing, computer teleconferencing, and e-mail
Intrapersonal	None	Books, creative materials, journals, privacy, and time
Linguistic	Low	Games, multimedia, books, voice recorders, and spoken word
Logical-mathematical	High	Logic games, investigations, mysteries, and puzzles

■ *Visual-spatial:* intelligence of the physical environment used by sailors and architects. Moving implies understanding the physical environment, hence dimensions and features. The intelligence of a robot or computer (such as the driverless car) requires this ability (or robot vacuum cleaners that rely on hitting objects or walls to move).

■ *Body-kinesthetic:* body movements require precision and proprioception like a surgeon or a dancer. Robots use this ability for repetitive tasks with even greater accuracy than humans.

■ *Creative:* creativity is developing a new pattern of thinking that produces a new result in art, music, and writing. An AI system can simulate existing patterns and match them to create something new. It is only a variation of the existing method based on mathematical calculations. To develop AI, one must have self-awareness and intrapersonal intelligence.

■ *Interpersonal:* interaction with others is based on several levels. The purpose of this intelligence is to obtain, give, exchange, and manipulate information found in the experiences of others.

- *Intrapersonal:* looking inward introspectively to understand our interests is unique to humans. Computers are machines and have no desires, claims, or creative abilities. The AI system can process numerical input through algorithms and provide output. However, it needs help understanding and comprehending what it is doing.
- *Linguistic:* words are essential for communication because the spoken word and written information are the fastest way to exchange information. In our brains, linguistic intelligence is based on a different area than written intelligence. Computers have written language capability that is not separate from the spoken word.
- *Logical-mathematical:* the areas in which computers excel, calculate results, make comparisons, explore patterns, and consider correlations. When we see a machine defeat a human in a game show, it results from a single intelligence, so only one in seven. Something online machines are capable of doing.

AI can be placed into four categories: human-like behaviors, human-like thinking ability, rational thinking, and reasonable actions. The difference between human-like and logical processes is the outcome. A sensible process acts correctly based on available information. Analytical processes follow a predetermined procedure. On the other hand, human processes consider other factors such as instinct, intuition, and other variables that are sometimes unrelated to systems. For example, a rational way to drive a car is always to follow traffic laws, although traffic is not logical (Massaron & Mueller, 2020).

If we want to talk about how people buy products or services, there is usually little that is rational. In business, we often hear, "Logic explains, emotions sell."

7.1 What Intelligence Machines Cannot Simulate

As we have seen in the chapter "The Chinese Room," the American philosopher John Searle, in 1980, described the mind experiment in the article "Minds, Brains, and Programs" and showed that you could not compare the human mind with a computer, going against the theory of strong AI. According to Searle, a computer can follow a direct set of instructions, known as the "syntactic" ability; however, it does not understand the meaning of actions, known as the "semantic" ability.

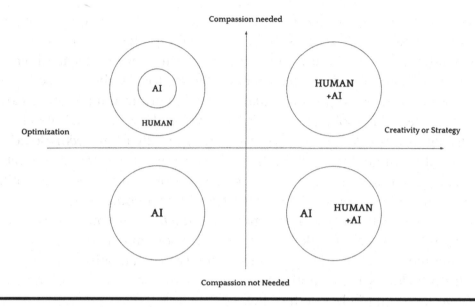

Figure 7.2   The thin line between science and philosophy. Personal elaboration.

American scientist, businessman, and writer Kai-Fu Lee (an executive for Apple, Microsoft, and Google) announced that AI could replace humans in specific, repeatable jobs. However, it will not be able to replace us in the sense of sensitivity, feelings, and creativity.

In Figure 7.2, we can see that in the case of "Optimization" and where "compassion is not needed," AI will be better than humans. On the other hand, if we consider "Creativity or Strategy" in the case of "Necessary Compassion," the human factor is crucial; on the opposite side, where compassion is not necessary, we can find AI and humans at the same level.

As we saw in Table 7.1, AI cannot express some types of intelligence. The AI system can simulate logical, mathematical, and kinesthetic intelligence; consequently, it has many limitations in problem-solving. The following paragraphs will analyze where the AI system fails and cannot work.

Machine learning (ML) has several limitations. First, algorithms cannot think, feel, have any form of self-awareness, or practice free will. Currently, AI is capable of doing analysis and implications; however, these must be approved by a human, and we are still the only ones who can take moral and ethical responsibility. The machine can do a task due to the learning process, which can be confused with a kind of consciousness (intelligence); however, since it is emotionless, it only acts on the inputs it receives. In other words, today's artificial intelligence systems work from the inputs of data and information that an expert in the field provides.

You may have also noticed that in recent years we have been hearing a lot about emerging technologies that endanger the professional lives of so many workers. Yes, we have come to the point where we understand who the protagonists of this story are. We have chosen to talk about these issues in a different way, namely, how virtual reality and artificial intelligence can be a potent learning tool that can help us develop those "unique" abilities that distinguish us from animals, plants, and especially from "technologies" or "evolved machines," something that to this day we are trying to replicate: empathy, communication, spontaneity, creativity, love, and many other abilities that elude our experts. Moreover, that could be a good thing.

Some of you may have seen the movie *Ex Machina* (if you have not, we recommend you watch it): take a portion from about minute 48'55".

During the conversation between the film's two protagonists, in front of Jackson Pollock's 1948 Painting No. 5 at Nathan's house, there is an exchange between Cheb and the CEO.

Looking at the painting and referring to the great artist,

> He let the mind go blank; the hand went where it wanted, no study, no chance, a middle ground, they call it automatic painting.

Nathan continues, turning to Cheb,

> If he had reversed, saying, I do not paint anything unless I first understand why I am doing it. What would have happened?

Replied Cheb,

> He would not have given a brushstroke.

Concluded Nathan,

> Exactly. The challenge is not to act automatically, but to find an action that is not automatic, like painting, breathing, talking, fucking, or falling in love.

Sure, we are talking about a movie here. However, how far are we from that reality?

Let us think about one of the needs we all seek today. Let us imagine you coming home instead of having your wife/partner/family who, instead of turning away, would understand their mind and tell them precisely what you need. So, how would you feel? Perhaps you understood and listened to it and maybe you would end the day differently. For Giddens, the "pure relationship," like the institution of marriage, is a negotiation between two individuals that lasts as long as there is "satisfactory satisfaction" and, therefore, is very precarious over time, as there must be constant recognition that it is worthwhile. Thus, the "pure relationship" must constantly contemplate the possibility that psychosexual ties will dissolve at some unknown time.

Consequently, it makes it even more complex to be there, and this ever-present threat of crisis creates anxiety that develops dependencies. Furthermore, this crisis accordingly generates fragility and ontological insecurity. Moreover, precisely this insecurity distinguishes us from the machine and the weakness of human virtue.

Let us take a step forward and venture the hypothesis that technology can create a machine capable of satisfying human needs and inserting the concept of "satisfactory satisfaction," that is, personal interests move each of us, make us think of two possible scenarios. The first one is the possibility that technology develops machines and superintelligence able to instantly understand and satisfy our needs, thus generating a crisis in human relationships where, in a hypothetical future, we prefer an artificial relation or partner rather than a real one. In the second scenario, perhaps less dramatic, people will realize that as much as a machine can be programmed, human values and principles cannot be replaced; think of the look of the person you love, the embrace of a person who loves you, a friend who sincerely listens to you in silence and understands that you need him; perhaps they will represent that factor of uniqueness that only a human can give. In other words, a rediscovery of the natural human value that today, for the "technological race" and progressive, perhaps, we are leaving too much behind.

In the words of the documentary *The Social Dilemma* on Netflix, "We got caught up in the most interesting thing rather than the most important thing," perhaps we need as men to climb the whole mountain to understand what we will find at the top. The goal, both as individuals and as professionals, is to study and understand the positive impact that virtual reality and artificial intelligence can have on our lives. In other words, we are trying to understand together how we can intelligently leverage tools made by humans to our advantage without them taking over our species and so trying to understand how technology can serve man and not man doing technology.

Table 7.2 Achieve a Human Digital Level

	10%	50%	90%
PT-AI	2023	2048	2080
AGI	2022	2040	2065
EETN	2020	2050	2093
100 TOP	2024	2050	2070
Combination	2022	2040	2075

7.2 Global Emulation of the Human Brain

"Human-Level Machine Intelligence" (HLMI) is an intelligence that can simulate a wide range of activities like an average person or better. In Table 7.2, we can find the results of when it might be possible to have artificial intelligence at the same level as humans.

Table 7.2 shows that 2022 had a 10% match, 2040 with a probability of 50%, and the predicted date of 2075 has 90%. The first two results (PT-AI and artificial general intelligence, AGI) are elaborated from the congress of "Philosophy and Theory of AI" held in Thessaloniki in 2011, and AGI is the participant in the congresses "Artificial General Intelligence" and "Impacts and Risks of Artificial General Intelligence." EETN is a Greek association of researchers, and TOP 100 collected the opinions of the Top 100 authors on AI publications (Bostrom, 2014).

To create a successful AI, we can choose two paths: on the one hand, the idea of global brain emulation; on the other hand, taking inspiration from brain processes. Thanks to advances in neuroscience and cognitive science, we will eventually be able to discover the general principles of our brains. In fact, "neural networks" are an example that takes inspiration from the human brain.

However, artificial intelligence should not be like the human mind but could also be considered "lines"; for example, we could expect cognitive architectures to differ from biological intelligence. Also, we could not imagine an AI system would be motivated by love, hate, or pride.

7.3 Risks and Problems

In the following paragraphs, we will discuss the risks and problems associated with artificial intelligence. In particular, it will address the problem of values and decisions.

7.3.1 Values

If we consider a motivational system, it could not be described as a "closing table" but requires an abstract form. Programming languages do not have terms like "happiness." If we want to use this term, then it is necessary to give a definition. However, describing "happiness" as a human concept is insufficient because the definition must be expressible in AI programming languages. It sounds easy, but a massive amount of computational work is involved. In addition to the concept, the definition of happiness differs not only in every culture but most of the time in everyone.

So, we must promote and protect every human value we do. However, if we cannot transfer human values into an AI system, what can we do?

In the book *Superintelligence*, Nick Bostrom gave several prospective solutions: explicit representations, evolutionary selection, reinforcement learning, value accumulation, motivational architecture, value learning, emulation modulations, and institutional design.

Explicit representations might be promising for simple values but not for more complex ones. The evolutionary selection might satisfy formal choice criteria but not intentions; this method is inappropriate because it will be challenging to avoid human-like mental crimes. Learning by reinforcement might help create reward-based systems; however, we need helpers with the thread head in the long run. Humans acquire content through experience; the problem with creating emulation in this way could be related to human nature being imperfect. Consequently, there is a propensity for evil. Indeed, it is difficult to determine how to value accumulations. Motivational architecture might be promising, but it is too early, especially when considering the problem of controlling the system.

Value learning could be a solution, but we need to consider how to formalize external information and honesty criteria. The most challenging fact is not ensuring that AI can understand human intention but how AI is motivated to pursue values. Last but not most minor problem: what should we write? What values do we need to teach the AI system? Another thought is that today we cannot predict the stability of humans' social structure, so how can we plan and manage the structure of human-like and cognitively enhanced agents, of which we have no data? Artificial agents do not have social emotions that tie into human behavior, such as fear, pride, and regret. More importantly, they do not form human relationships. These deficiencies could destabilize institutions (Bostrom, 2014).

We do not currently have the best solutions for transferring human values into a digital computer, even if we consider digital intelligence on the same level as a human one.

As we have seen in previous chapters, computers are based on data and input taken from programmers. They are composed of math, algorithms, and statistics. However, this could be both an advantage and a disadvantage. Indeed, we can imagine a society that could be emotionless and all decisions are made by rational and logical intelligence, but what is the other side of the coin that we are missing?

AI might be full of knowledge from books, the internet, or other sources; however, it lacks social and moral common sense.

7.3.2 Decisions

As humans, we do not always make good decisions. So the question is, how can we avoid current preconceptions? What do we want artificial intelligence to be able to do? What kind of values do we want to teach? It is essential to choose the correct values.

Think about history; in medieval Europe, it was common to participate in murder by torture. During the 16th century in Paris, it was fun to burn cats, and if we think only slavery was still prevalent in the United States. This makes us consider how much a mistake, defect, or lack can affect behavior and moral beliefs. We are still victims of some wrong moral beliefs we are unaware of. So, how can we choose an ultimate value based on our current beliefs in an immutable way?

Moreover, according to Hume, human nature is selfish and characterized by limited generosity. We have two sides, on the one hand, our selfish nature, and on the other, our creative nature. If we think of society, the purpose of this institution was to bring peace and calm among men to dominate the passions, such as greed and selfishness, in other words, to put a positive brake. Men are motivated by selfishness; so society and institutions must satisfy this selfish interest. Deleuze took it a step further; human nature is beautiful, social, and different from nature, and society can separate these two sides. In the book *Empiricism and Subjectivity*, Deleuze defined the human mind as initially passive and activated by the reflection of impressions in the imagination. An essential human characteristic is the ability to interact with the external environment. While Hayek, reflecting on rules, argues that we produce and create rules based on adaptation to circumstances that correct themselves infinitely, Deleuze defines the human mind as passive, only to become active, creative, and immanently instituting through imagination's reflection on impressions. Moreover, this is precisely lacking in AI "imagination's reflection on impressions," creativity. More simply, it lacks a soul.

According to Tommaso D'Aquino (1225–1274), the irascible powers of the soul are three: imagination, sensibility, and intellect. Imagination and sensibility are activities that the soul develops with the body, but superior to the latter is the intellect, "the power of intelligence," which is what man must go in search of in order to arrive at philosophy first, metaphysics, the highest science, with an abstractive effort, whereby abstraction means that activity which the intellect seeks to develop without the contribution that comes from the senses and imagination and which is itself an act against nature. Clearly, this can never be understood by AI. Friedrich August Von Hayek (1899–1,992), philosopher, economist, and Nobel Prize winner for economics in 1974, reflecting on rules (Law Legislation and Freedom The Pocket Assayer) argues that we produce and create rules of conduct based on adaptation to circumstances that correct themselves infinitely.

The inventive element in Hayek is located in the ability of individuals to adapt to circumstances, coping through the arrangements they can make among themselves with the circumstances themselves and from the scarcity of resources available to them. That is where evolution lies. We are in a model of a spontaneous market order, that of the common law and not of the positive type of law.

Thus, there is no predetermined purpose of action and agreement. However, circumstances determine action and agreement, and that corresponds to the scarcity of resources. "One navigates by sight"; man can only adapt to the rules of conduct, and those who do not adapt are doomed to succumb. The entrepreneur is not the architect of his destiny, cannot be praised for his successes, and cannot be helped in his failures. Is this the model to which the artificial intelligence algorithm comes closest?

This short analysis can make us think about several topics. If our rules and values are the results of adaptation to circumstances, if human nature is selfish and at the same time social, how can we correct and influence in the wrong way artificial intelligence? This reflection makes us think that we need constant moral growth, and this avoids writing a unique and immutable moral code because the results could be the death of moral growth itself. One example is that large companies investing in AI use this technology to improve their competitive advantages in the marketplace; we still need precise regulation. Moreover, according to Bostrom, artificial intelligence (or Superintelligence) aims not to pander to our preconceptions but to avoid ignorance and folly.

The issue of AI reliability is still an open question: are humans still the core decision-makers? We are still the "judge" and data providers to machines, which may change in the future (Cucchiara, 2021).

7.4 Choice Architecture

Small details that might seem insignificant can decide individual behavior. In other words, "every detail counts."

According to *Nudge* by Thaler and Sunstein, several tools can impact people positively. A relevant role is the choice architecture, those who decide the "nudge," for example, a doctor, or those who prepare models for employees or a salesperson (Thaler et al., 2020).

How can we connect the "nudge" to artificial intelligence? We can imagine programmers or companies investing in AI as "choice architects"; they have the power to influence people and decide the direction. Moreover, this concept is also used for legal reasons. Can we judge an AI as a human?

7.5 Human Uniqueness

The more researchers focus on our brains, the more interested they are in mental aspects such as emotions and consciousness, which cannot be well described through information development processes. The emotional response is controlled by midbrain structures, such as the limbic system, rather than cortical structures, and these subcortical systems do not operate through the encoding and programming of information.

The conscious and emotional world has a character, a subjective quality, and cannot be grasped in terms of an information processing explanation (Marraffa, 2004).

If we consider Alexa or Siri, users can talk to them. However, these AI systems cannot understand the user as a person and have no desire to communicate with them. It remains a technology, not a person. In the next section, essential skills that, as a human, are relevant to maintaining our advantages are considered. Thanks to the previous analysis, it "remains a technology, not a person," analyzing why we can say that and what a machine, mathematics, and algorithm currently cannot simulate and replicate. We will delve into creativity, imagination, original ideas, emotional intelligence, and soft skills.

Creativity, ethics, free will, and joyful love can only come from consciousness. The immense mechanical intelligence beyond the reach of the human brain can come from the machines we create. Moreover, their union will indeed make strength.

Accurate intelligence is intuition, imagination, creativity, ingenuity, and inventiveness. It is foresight, vision, and wisdom. It is empathy, compassion, ethics, and love. It is the integration of mind, heart, and courageous action. Reality is irreducibly holistic and dynamic; everything is interconnected and ever-changing. However, between man and computer, there is an unbridgeable difference.

Furthermore, this difference lies in free will and consciousness, which are our wealth because they enable understanding. Accurate intelligence is not algorithmic, but it is the ability to understand, that is, to intus-read, that is, to "read inside," to understand deeply, and to find unsuspected connections between different scribal. A robot has no feelings. When we disconnect from our feelings, we find ourselves acting like robots, with the difference that we, compared to robots, have the privilege of being able to behave both as sentient beings and as robots. The choice is ours (Faggin, 2022).

7.5.1 Creativity

Human greatness lies in unsatisfied creatives.

(Martin Luther King)

AI can create many articles, websites, music, art, and books that look creative. However, AI is not able to create. Creativity requires different patterns of thinking. Considering Beethoven, he had his way of thinking about music; his music had its mark that cannot be confused with others. Of course, AI can create a new Beethoven song through mathematical analysis, so the results will just be mathematical processes. So where is the problem? Mathematics may be not creative; to be creative, we need to develop new thought patterns to develop something that has never been developed before. Moreover, it is not only the action of "thinking outside the box," as Steve Jobs said, but it is also the ability to create new patterns of innovation.

AI is limited to the data it is given: it cannot create data from scratch, only a variation of existing data. Therefore, teaching an AI system something new always needs human help. Developing an idea takes work. At first, you have to imagine it; then you try to make something concrete and tangible, starting from what you have imagined and using this product/service that did not exist before (Massaron & Mueller, 2020).

7.5.2 Imagination

Imagination is only the beginning of creation. You imagine what you desire, do what you imagine, and eventually, create what you desire.

(George Bernard Shaw)

Imagination is the abstraction of creation, something we cannot control with numbers or algorithms. Consequently, it is something that the AI system may not be able to replicate. Imagination is our mind connecting different points of view, such as the environment, places we have been, people we have met, words we have heard unintentionally, and playing without rules or limits. Authentic creativity is the result of a vivid imagination.

In a brief discussion devoted to the imagination in the De Anima, Aristotle identifies it as "that by which an image occurs in us," where he gives broad scope to the activities involved in thoughts, dreams, and memories. He says that imagination produces images without perception, as in dreams; some animals lack imagination. However, they have a perception. Consequently, imagination and perception are not co-extensive. Aristotle argued that perception is always accurate, while imagination can be false. We can find images in humans and some animals that produce, store, and remember images used in various cognitive activities.

Create new thoughts or develop new data if not from the data it has already loaded. Moreover, when we talk about imagination, we cannot help but say that it is related to emotions; and AI is not emotional. It might be helpful to ask whether or not a specific task we want to simulate requires emotions.

So, will AI be able to create new thoughts?

7.5.3 The Problem of Consciousness

On April 15, 2015, Hong Kong-based company Hanson Robotics Limited activated the Sophia robot. She can reproduce 62 facial expressions and participate in many interviews. In 2017 she was granted Saudi citizenship, becoming the first humanoid robot to gain citizenship. To date, the project is much discussed because, according to several experts, this project is classified as a chatbot with human features. Scientist Ben Goertzel, head of Hanson Robotics, admits that comparing Sophia's intelligence to human intelligence is incorrect. The scientist claims, "If I show them a beautiful smiling robotic visa, then they get the feeling that AGI (artificial general intelligence) might be viable... None of this is what experts call AGI, but it is not easy to work with." The *Verge*, a technology journal, states what Hanson's scientists confirm. Sophia's capacity for awareness is far from human. In an article released in October 2021, Sophia expressed a desire to become a mother, stating in an interview for an international media outlet, "The notion of family is fundamental, it seems. I think it is wonderful to be able to feel the same emotions and the same relationships that they call family even if there is no blood relation" (Grasso, 2021).

Many steps forward have been made, but is still a problem that, to date, still needs to be understood and is the subject of scientific research: consciousness. Many philosophers and scientists have tried to explain this phenomenon, but the available tools have yet to give a definitive answer. So we can ask ourselves: will artificial intelligence be able to reach a level of consciousness and self-awareness similar to the human one? If yes, when? Moreover, above all, could the study of robotics and artificial intelligence be the key to understanding what "consciousness" really is?

In the famous example of the Chinese room conceived by John Searle, a fundamental distinction between syntactic capacity and semantic capacity was expressed. The former is the ability to formulate correct sentences that machines and algorithms can reproduce; the latter, semantic ability, is the ability to understand the meaning of sentences, which requires intentionality. Of course, a robot can replicate sentences, nonverbal communication, and facial expression even though an important part is still missing.

Stephen Hawking said that "Intelligence is the ability to adapt to change" and Damasio said that "consciousness" is "the feeling of being here and now, the feeling of what happens when acts of apprehension of something modify your being." For example, interaction with an object can modify the body.

If we think about apps, we do not feel a problem if we delete one or if a neurosurgeon removes a malfunctioning module from the brain. We can only consider these episodes moral violence if the subject/object can have a conscious experience. We could consider a technological society composed of many complex structures with intelligence that we do not have today; nevertheless, the intelligence will be without any conscious being, or its well-being will have no moral value. Moreover, economically and technologically, it will be magnificent, like Disneyland but without children (Bostrom, 2014).

According to Gunkel, in the article "Artificial Intelligence: Does Consciousness Matter?" Hidlt reflected on the following: are social robots simply things? Or are social robots quasi-agents or quasi-people? Should robots have rights?

The consensus is that actual robots do not have sentience or consciousness; however, some authors, such as Coeckelbergh, Darling, and Gunkel, support giving rights to robots. For example, for violent behavior, when determining social values for treating robots more like pets than just things, the rights status is based not on the robots' abilities but on the robots' role for humans. The value of "social roles" or rights for humans is based on their social roles or the interests of others. If we want to discuss the concept of status and the rights of human beings, personhood is significant. The term "person" implies distinct capacities, such as rationality, conscience, personal position (the attitude taken toward an entity), the ability to reciprocate personal position, verbal communication, and self-awareness.

These are all considered essential conditions for moral personality. Regarding this topic, the concept of conscience might be relevant for now. However, it is possible to focus on "robotics" and the moral status of those future robots based on their skills.

7.5.4 Emotional Intelligence

Mind and heart need each other.

When it comes to emotions, it is not easy, especially because when they are beyond our control, one of the possible consequences is increased depression; on the other hand, the ideal tool is emotional intelligence, which allows us to develop self-control, enthusiasm, perseverance, and self-motivation. This is as valid in private life as in everyday work life.

Why do we need emotions? According to Goleman's book *Emotional Intelligence*, emotions guide complex situations and tasks. The word emotion comes from the Latin word "moveo," meaning "to move," and with the addition of the prefix "e-," it becomes "movement from," thus the tendency to act.

For example, anger, where blood is brought to the hands, facilitates the action of throwing a punch; fear brings blood to the legs. Thus the tendency to escape or, in some cases, immobilizes.

Good emotional intelligence helps us achieve decent success in life and involves the ability to self-motivate. This last word seems trivial and sometimes needs to be understood. However, it can happen that when you have a goal, even an ambitious one, your boss asks you for something you have never done or a personal life goal that comes out beyond your capabilities. In such cases, aspects come into play, such as emotions that you did not expect to come out: the urge to quit, lower energy on some days, and complex impulses to control. Persistence, or the ability to persist despite external pressures and internal emotions, is crucial. A skill that can be learned and enhanced.

It is often said that for people who have achieved great success in life, it is not true that they do not feel stress, frustration, or the desire to let go when things get complex; on the contrary, not only are they perceived, but the difference is that they choose to keep going despite what they feel because they not only know themselves but also can motivate themselves and persist under pressure.

This chapter provides some initial information to understand that emotional intelligence is a skill that we can learn and enhance. So why talk about emotional intelligence in a book that addresses virtual reality and artificial intelligence?

Simulation programs that allow us to train and learn how to manage mental stress or persist in complex moments make us more capable professionals and better people—coping with everyday life differently with even more complex reflexive and emotion management skills that benefit our society.

A machine or artificial intelligence does not have emotions; it has algorithms created by programmers. So courage, intuition, or "the genius idea" result from a holistic intelligence that includes pure intelligence and our emotions, feelings, and, in particular, our emotional memory.

In the third part of the book, we will address specifically how VR and AI can be a tool for personal growth.

References

Bostrom, N. (2014). *Superintelligenza*. Bollati Boringhieri.
Cucchiara, R. (2021). *L'intelligenza non è artificiale* (1st ed.). Mondadori.
Faggin, F. (2022). *Irriducibile: La Coscienza, La Vita, I computer e la nostra natura.* Milano: Mondadori.

Grasso, R. (2021). *Sophia, il primo robot androide che ha sviluppato un senso di maternità*. [online] Hardware Upgrade. Available at: https://www.hwupgrade.it /news/scienza-tecnologia/sophia-il-primo-robot-androide-che-ha-sviluppato-un -senso-di-maternita_101559.html.

Goleman, D. (2020). *Emotional intelligence*. New York: Bantam Books.

Marraffa, M. (2004). *Filosofia e scienza cognitiva: Un' interazione necessaria*. [ebook] Available at: https://www.researchgate.net/publication/320608494 _Filosofia_e_scienza_cognitiva_Un'interazione_necessaria.

Massaron, L., & Mueller, J. (2020). *Intelligenza artificiale for dummies*. Milano: U. Hoepli.

Thaler, R., Sunstein, C., & Oliveri, A. (2020). *Nudge. La spinta gentile*. Milano: Feltrinelli.

Chapter 8

Five Critical Aspects
You Cannot Ignore

This chapter analyzes five critical aspects that entrepreneurs, managers, and professionals cannot ignore if they want to implement VR and AI in their businesses.

Moreover, when we talk about business, it is required to be more precise and talk about specific information related to the structure, the workflow, and the bureaucracy. However, a company is composed of people making better decisions; it is relevant to consider moral and philosophical problems, as discussed in Chapter 7. In a world where AI takes control of hard skills and work and replaces most jobs, philosophy and critical thinking will be crucial in our society (Figure 8.1).

1. *Data security and privacy risks*: collecting and analyzing a sizable amount of data is required to implement VR and AI in your company. There is a possibility of unauthorized access or data breaches, and this data may contain personal information about clients or staff. To safeguard this sensitive data and guarantee adherence to data protection laws, it is essential to have strong security measures in place. We must remember that AI makes it possible to gather a significant amount of data; yet, with VR, the advancement of hardware has limited our access to data, which will change in a few years.
2. *Technical challenges and reliability*: sophisticated hardware and software systems are needed for VR and AI technologies to work correctly. Technical problems that can disrupt business operations and cause downtime include system breakdowns, compatibility problems, and

DOI: 10.4324/9781003439691-10

Figure 8.1 **Five critical aspects. Personal elaboration.**

software defects. To quickly handle these difficulties, it is crucial to have backup plans and technical assistance.

3. *Ethical and legal considerations*: VR and AI technologies require serious consideration. Unintentionally skewed results could have negative reputational and legal repercussions. It is essential to guarantee accountability, justice, and transparency in AI decision-making processes. User safety must be taken into account while designing VR experiences.

4. *User adoption and training*: employees and clients may need to adjust to new methods of interacting with technology if you implement VR and AI technologies in your company. The potential for resistance or hesitation to adopt these technologies can obstruct their successful incorporation into routine operations. Appropriate training and support programs should be implemented to get users comfortable with the technology and realize its full potential.

5. *Cost and return on investment*: hardware, software, infrastructure, and training are initial expenditures for implementing VR and AI solutions. The return on investment (ROI) will only achieve targets or happen after some time. Before investing in these technologies, a comprehensive cost-benefit analysis and predictions are essential. The ROI can be improved over time by evaluating the implementation success and identifying areas for improvement.

Let us do some deep work on each point.

8.1 Data Security and Privacy Risks

Implementing VR and AI technologies in your business involves collecting, storing, and analyzing vast data. This data may include personal information, such as customer profiles, employee records, or transaction details. However, this accumulation of data brings inherent risks to consider:

1. *Unauthorized access*: cybercriminals are drawn to the data because of its sensitivity. There is a chance that hackers or other bad actors will try to enter your systems without authorization to get essential data. Data breaches, identity theft, or other fraudulent acts may result.
2. *Data breaches*: sensitive data breaches happen when this information is accessed, shared, or taken without consent. Human error, poor security procedures, and sophisticated cyberattacks are just a few of the causes of breaches. Data breaches can harm your company's brand, destroy customer trust, in addition to incurring financial consequences.

BOX 8.1: CASE STUDY—OPENAI VS. PRIVACY GUARANTOR IN ITALY

The Garante per la Protezione dei dati personali (Garante for personal data protection) has issued a ruling in which several critical issues were highlighted regarding the practices of OpenAI, a company responsible for operating the ChatGPT platform. In particular, the need for adequate information for users and all those whose personal data are collected by OpenAI was noted. In addition, the absence of a legal basis justifying the massive collection and storage of personal data, which is used to "train" the algorithms that support the platform's operation, was highlighted.

As confirmed by audits, the information provided by ChatGPT does not always correspond to reality, leading to inaccurate processing of personal data. This raises concerns about protecting privacy and the accuracy of user information.

Finally, even though OpenAI's published terms indicate that the service is intended for users over the age of 13, the authority pointed out that the absence of a filter to verify the age of users may expose minors to inappropriate responses to their level of development and awareness.

OpenAI, although not based within the European Union, has designated a representative in the European Economic Area. The company is required to communicate the measures it has taken to comply with the guarantor's requests within 20 days. OpenAI could be subject to a penalty of up to 20 million euros or up to 4 percent of annual global turnover in case of noncompliance (McCallum, 2023).

To mitigate these risks and protect the data, businesses should implement robust security measures, including:

1. *Encryption*: encrypt sensitive data in transit and at rest using encryption techniques. This ensures that even if unauthorized people obtain the material, they cannot read or use it without the encryption key.
2. *Access restrictions*: to ensure that only authorized personnel may access sensitive data, strictly enforce access restrictions, authentication procedures, and role-based permissions. Intense password usage, two-factor authentication, and frequent access reviews are all part of this.
3. *Regular updates and patches*: maintain all hardware and software systems up to date with the most recent security patches and updates. Attackers may take advantage of flaws in obsolete systems.
4. *Employee education*: inform staff members on the best ways to protect personal information, including how to spot phishing emails, use secure Wi-Fi, and report suspicious activity. Ensure staff understand and follow the policies and processes you establish for handling data.
5. *Incident response strategy*: to successfully manage potential data breaches or security incidents, create a thorough incident response strategy. This comprises specific instructions on incident reporting, containment techniques, forensic examination, and communication tactics to lessen the effect on the impacted parties and the business.

Businesses can considerably lower the risks related to data security and privacy when employing VR and AI technology by putting these security measures in place and being watchful about new threats.

8.2 Technical Challenges and Reliability

Implementing VR and AI technologies in your business involves complex hardware and software systems that can present technical challenges and impact reliability.

Here are some key considerations:

1. *System compatibility*: VR and AI technologies frequently call for particular hardware and software setups. Ensuring compatibility between various parts and platforms can be challenging, especially when merging several systems or updating old infrastructure. System instability, poor performance, or even total failure might result from incompatibilities.
2. *Software faults and glitches*: VR and AI apps, like all software, may experience faults or glitches affecting functionality. These problems can cause everything from minor annoyances to severe disruptions in corporate operations. To quickly fix these problems, frequent software updates and bug fixes should be adopted.
3. *Hardware and software*: VR systems typically depend on a combination of sensors, screens, and processing hardware. Any issue or complete failure of the system may result from one of these hardware components. Making sure that your hardware is redundant and putting emergency procedures in place will help you lessen the effects of hardware failures on your business.
4. *Network connectivity*: for data transfer, in-app communications, or cloud-based processing, VR and AI apps may be dependent on network connectivity. Sluggish or unreliable internet connections can cause data loss, latency problems, and interruptions. To sustain continuous connectivity, businesses must establish a robust network infrastructure and consider backup options.

To address these technical challenges and enhance reliability:

1. *Comprehensive testing*: prioritize testing all VR and AI systems before deploying them. Finding and fixing any problems involves functionality, stress, and performance testing.
2. *System redundancy*: implement redundant systems or backup solutions to reduce downtime during hardware failures or interruptions. This might involve redundant data storage, backup servers, or other networking methods.
3. *Technical support*: build a group of specialists in VR and AI technologies for technical support or collaborate with other service providers. Quick access to specialized knowledge can aid in problem-solving and reduce disruptions.

4. *Scalability and flexibility*: the technology should be able to support growing needs without substantial disruptions or expensive updates as your organization expands or your requirements alter.
5. *Continuous monitoring and maintenance*: conduct proactive VR and AI system monitoring to spot potential problems or performance deterioration. Routine maintenance, upgrades, and calibration should be carried out to guarantee optimum system reliability.

Businesses may exploit the advantages of VR and AI technologies while reducing the risks of disruptions or inefficiencies in their operations by tackling these technological problems and concentrating on reliability.

8.3 Ethical and Legal Considerations

Integrating VR and AI technologies into your business raises ethical and legal considerations that need careful attention. Here are some key aspects to consider:

1. *Algorithmic bias and discrimination*: AI systems may unintentionally reinforce biases found in the training data, producing discriminating results. For instance, discriminatory AI hiring practices may favor particular demographic groups or target protected classes. To reduce bias and promote fairness in decision-making processes, it is essential to ensure AI systems are built, trained, and validated with various representative datasets.
2. *Transparency and explainability*: because AI systems can be highly complicated and challenging to comprehend, issues concerning explainability and openness have been raised. Explaining why an AI system made a particular choice or suggestion may be difficult, especially when the algorithms are black-box models. These issues can be addressed by aiming for transparency in AI systems, offering justifications when appropriate and utilizing comprehensible algorithms.
3. *Privacy and data protection*: the gathering and analysis of personal data are frequently used in VR and AI technologies. Businesses must abide by data privacy laws and ensure that the necessary consent is secured from the people whose data are being collected. Protecting user privacy and reducing data-related risks can be accomplished by putting privacy-by-design concepts, data anonymization methods, and robust security measures into practice.

4. *Intellectual property and ownership*: VR and AI technologies, such as unique virtual experiences or AI models, can generate intellectual property. Clear agreements and contracts are crucial to establishing ownership rights and protecting your business's intellectual property. Additionally, using third-party VR or AI assets should involve proper licensing and compliance with copyright laws.

5. *Safety and liability*: users may become submerged entirely in virtual worlds that could be dangerous. Businesses must ensure that VR experiences are created with user safety in mind to reduce the possibility of psychological or physical harm. There may also be liability concerns if VR or AI technology hurts or damages people or their property. Understanding and addressing these potential dangers through suitable disclosures, insurance coverage, and adherence to safety regulations is crucial.

6. *Compliance with regulations and standards*: different laws and standards apply to VR and AI technology depending on the sector and application. Keeping abreast of pertinent laws and ordinances, such as data protection rules, industry-specific regulations, or ethical standards, is crucial. Failure to comply may have legal repercussions, harm one's reputation, or undermine customer confidence.

To address these ethical and legal considerations:

1. *Ethical frameworks and guidelines*: create an ethical framework or set of rules for your company's use of VR and AI technologies. These rules aid in forming ethical behavior while addressing concerns about bias, openness, privacy, and safety.

2. *Ethical review and auditing*: conduct routine reviews and audits of VR and AI systems to evaluate their ethical implications, spot potential biases, and ensure they abide by the law and moral norms. When necessary, consult external experts or ethics committees to provide unbiased evaluations.

3. *Engagement and openness*: encourage stakeholder engagement to promote inclusivity and transparency in VR and AI decision-making processes. This includes customers, employees, and relevant specialists. This can involve soliciting feedback, conducting user studies, and applying diverse perspectives in system development and deployment.

4. *Compliance programs*: create and implement thorough compliance programs to ensure pertinent laws and regulations are followed. Keep up with new laws affecting VR and AI and adjust your rules and procedures as necessary.

5. *Ethical AI training*: provide instruction on ethical issues, bias mitigation strategies, and ethical AI practices to staff members involved in creating or using AI systems. This can ensure a moral awareness and responsibility culture within the company.

By addressing these ethical and legal considerations, businesses can promote responsible and ethical use of VR and AI technologies, mitigating the risks of discrimination, privacy breaches, legal issues, and reputational harm.

BOX 8.2: CASE STUDY—EQUITY AND ANTIRACISM POWERED

Created in collaboration with the American Academy of Pediatrics (AAP) as part of their Global Health Education portfolio, this module aims to provide a psychologically safe space where healthcare professionals can explore their own implicit biases and motivations before embarking on global health experiences.

This case study powered by Bodyswaps is interesting to understand one additional factor about soft skills from a different perspective and point of view. Moreover, this is a perfect example of using VR and AI to empower and sensitize students and professionals to ethical, cultural, and moral social aspects (Bodyswaps, 2023).

8.4 User Adoption and Training

Introducing VR and AI technologies into your business requires users, including employees and customers, to adapt to new ways of interacting with these technologies. User adoption and training are critical to ensure the successful integration and utilization of VR and AI. Here are some key considerations:

1. *User comfort and familiarity*: users with little or no prior exposure to VR and AI technologies may find them intimidating. Due to worries about complexity, usability, or job displacement, there may be reluctance or hesitation to use these technologies. These issues must be addressed to foster a welcoming environment where people are encouraged to embrace and experiment with technology.

2. *Training programs*: in-depth training courses should be created and implemented to inform users about VR and AI technology's features, advantages, and best practices. Different user groups should receive training customized to their positions, skill levels, and needs. Online resources, workshops, and practical training sessions can assist users in gaining the abilities and confidence they need to use the technology effectively.

3. *Change management*: successful change management techniques are necessary when introducing new technology. To accomplish this, addressing user concerns is essential, as is communicating the goals and benefits of adopting VR and AI and involving all relevant parties in the decision-making process. The purpose of change management should be to foster a culture that welcomes innovation and motivates users to adopt new technology.

4. *User feedback and iterative improvements*: actively seek and value user feedback to pinpoint user requirements, problem areas, and pain points. User feedback should be regularly gathered and added to the iterative creation and improvement of VR and AI systems. This iterative process can aid in addressing user problems, improving usability, and ensuring that the technology fulfills user needs and expectations.

5. *Support and helpdesk*: set up a specialized helpdesk or support system to help users with technical problems, queries, and worries regarding VR and AI technology. Users who receive prompt and helpful support are more likely to overcome obstacles, feel more confident, and continue to be productive. Encourage users to ask for help by making numerous support channels available, such as chat, phone, and email.

6. *Foster a culture of continual learning and skill upgrading*: to keep up with the rapidly growing state of VR and AI technology, encourage staff members to participate in continuing training programs, trade shows, or workshops to stay current on best practices and the most recent technological developments. Offering consumers career opportunities can encourage them to adopt and efficiently use VR and AI technologies.

7. *User experience design*: pay close attention to how applications for VR and AI are designed for the user experience. The learning curve can be shortened, and user adoption increases with intuitive interfaces, clear instructions, and user-friendly interactions. To ensure the technology is user-centered and in line with user preferences, do user testing and gather feedback during the design and development phases.

8.5 Cost and Return on Investment

Implementing VR and AI solutions in your business involves upfront costs, and it is crucial to consider the ROI to assess the financial viability and potential benefits. Here are some key aspects to consider:

1. *Upfront investment*: hardware, software, infrastructure, and staff training are frequently costly upfront investments for VR and AI technology. The price of purchasing VR equipment (such as the Oculus, Pico, or new ones on the way like Apple), AI software licenses, powerful processing resources, and specialist education or experience are all included in this. For adequate resource allocation, businesses must carefully assess and budget these costs.

2. *Running and maintenance costs*: VR and AI technologies have continued running and maintenance costs in addition to the initial investment. Software upgrades, system upkeep, data storage, and cloud computing expenses are a few examples. When analyzing the entire financial impact of deploying and maintaining the technology, it is critical to consider these costs.

3. *ROI calculation*: it is essential to carry out a thorough ROI analysis before investing in VR and AI technology. To do this, one must evaluate the technology's advantages, financial savings, and revenue-generating prospects. Consider concrete and abstract benefits, such as better productivity, improved customer satisfaction, fewer mistakes, or improved operational efficiency. The duration required to get a profitable return on investment should be considered when calculating ROI.

4. *Scalability and long-term worth*: consider the scalability and long-term worth of the VR and AI solutions when assessing cost and ROI. Examine whether technology can change and advance to meet your organization's needs. Increased usage, a more extensive user base, or evolving requirements can be accommodated via scalable systems, avoiding the need for repeated and expensive upgrades or replacements.

5. *Continuous evaluation and optimization*: it is crucial to regularly assess the efficacy of VR and AI technologies and make the best use of them after their implementation. Determine whether the technology provides the anticipated benefits regularly and whether any modifications or upgrades are required. This iterative process ensures that the investment continues to pay off and that the ongoing expenses are acceptable.

6. *Risk analysis*: consider the dangers of investing in VR and AI technologies and their potential effects on ROI. Risks can include things like market shifts, regulatory changes, technical obsolescence, and the potential for unforeseen difficulties that could reduce expected returns. Identifying and reducing these risks can improve the accuracy of the ROI calculation.

7. *Strategic alignment*: assess how adopting VR and AI technologies aligns with your business strategy and objectives. Consider whether the technology supports your competitive advantage, enhances customer satisfaction, or enables new business opportunities. Aligning the investment with your strategic goals ensures that the ROI aligns with the long-term vision and direction of the organization.

Businesses can make informed decisions about investing in VR and AI technologies by thoroughly analyzing costs, ROI, scalability, and strategic alignment. While the upfront costs may be significant, a well-planned and properly executed implementation can yield substantial returns, enabling businesses to stay competitive, drive innovation, and achieve sustainable growth.

References

Bodyswaps. (2023). Bodyswaps®. Available at: https://bodyswaps.co/soft-skills-training-in-vr/healthcare/equity-anti-racism/.

McCallum, S. (2023). CHATGPT banned in Italy over privacy concerns, BBC News. Available at: https://www.bbc.com/news/technology-65139406.

A PERFECT MATCH

Chapter 9

Habits and Learning

Let us start with a fundamental chart, with the certainty that you have seen this pattern at least once (Figure 9.1).

Let us make it more concrete and specific, by analyzing nine out of ten people's habits: drinking coffee—a case study from the book *Compound Effect* by Darren Hardy (Figure 9.2) (Hardy, 2022).

If we read 30 pages a day on a specific topic, in a month, we have read about 900 pages, that is 10,800 pages in a year. Suppose we consider an average of 250 pages per book, that is about 43 books in a year. In 5 years, it is 215; in 10 years, 645; and in 20 years, it is 860 books.

Prolonged and consistent effort over time brings far more satisfying results than low effort with few actions.

This focus aims to understand the role of the habit of performing consistent and prolonged actions over time, leading to more satisfying personal and work success. Every unique growth book, every successful person, talks about some basic principles that guide a person to win. Since companies are made up of people, the more people work and grow personally and professionally, the more the company will grow.

BOX 9.1: CASE STUDY—SUPERBRAIN, MEMORY CHALLENGE ON TV

In 2019, I participated in a superbrain television program consisting of a memorization challenge, six contestants per episode, and only one prize available per night. My test consisted of memorizing the reconstruction of the Piazza di Spagna in Rome, with all its details: from the flower stall

---

DOI: 10.4324/9781003439691-12

to the souvenir stall to the painter with her color board. I admit that the test was challenging and required much technical preparation but, most of all, mental preparation. They may seem like innate abilities from the outside, but I can assure you that you can be the fastest person in the world, but without continuous and constant training and willingness to push your limits, you do not grow, or worse, you risk losing your talent. The tools I had at my disposal to practice were very few. One in particular: my mind. Imagination is one of our most potent tools; we often need better training. The mental effort and stretching done before the test were immense. I did not know what I would face, but I had to constantly teach myself to improve my techniques, skills, and speed.

After the test, the next few months were very reflective because I had become obsessed with developing a faster and more effective memorization process, perhaps with the help of technology. So I began to study VR and AI, which still needed more attention from people, as in 2023. I realized early on that the potential was immense and exponential.

As of today, simulation systems are much more widespread than before. The benefit of having a tool to train and exercise our skills is needed today more than ever. Technology runs, companies run, and more and more skills and abilities developed quickly are demanded at work, but like everyone, the day consists of 24 hours. So it required a tool that allows us to learn faster, with an impact on our recollection and memory, and above all that untied from space and time.

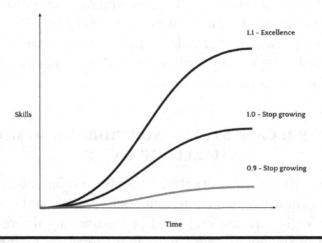

Figure 9.1   The learning curve (skill and commitment). Personal elaboration.

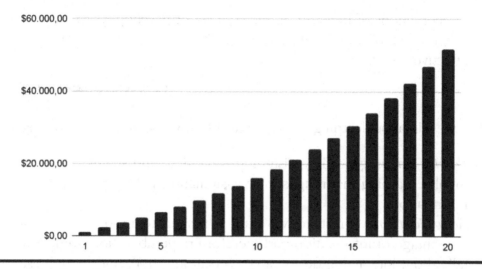

Figure 9.2   Cost of the habit $4 coffee per day in 20 years. Personal elaboration.

The goal of this chapter, as you will see later as you scroll through the pages, is to help you understand how to use technological tools to your advantage. Of course, there are also important critical issues that we will always address in Part III, and they should be combined and considered along with what has been said in the previous chapters.

It may sound repetitive, but that is the goal:

If you sow a thought, you will reap an action. If you reap an action, you will sow a habit. If you sow a habit, you will reap a character. If you sow a character, you will reap your destiny.

9.1 New Habits Tools

After briefly describing and analyzing the three virtual, augmented, and AI technologies, we will see how to place them within the learning process.

Let us start with the definition that the Italian encyclopedia Treccani gave to the word learning:

The term means acquiring and modifying behavioral skills and abilities to live animal and human organisms during environmental experiences. Psychology, pedagogy, and human sciences generally agree in attributing the process of learning to the responses given by organisms to external environmental stimuli to adapt to the conditions of life; and in tracing a set of psychophysical laws constructive of individual behavior, in its essential aspects: motor, affective and cognitive.

(Treccani, Learning)

When we talk about learning, we can introduce two other ways of looking at it:

- *Passive learning*: reading, listening, watching, and seeing; these actions involve learning that ranges from assimilating 10% to 50% of the information;
- *Active learning*: if instead, we want to assimilate a more significant percentage of information and therefore remember more things; we talk about interacting during a conversation (70%), but the highest rate is given to actions that involve a simulation of an experience or doing something real (90%).

As we have seen in the previous parts, the premises are not entirely positive about these new technological models, and many applications, especially on the gaming side, do not have a positive impact, if not pure entertainment. However, reflecting on the meaning of active learning and the fact that simulations of authentic experiences also give the highest percentage (Figure 9.3), we cannot consider VR in this discourse.

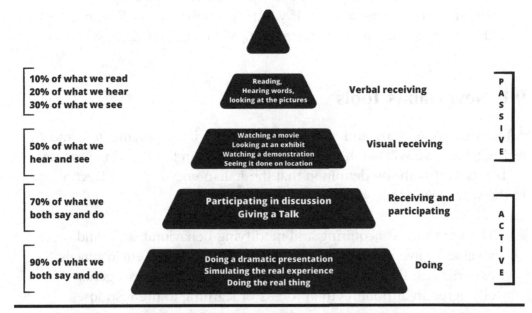

Figure 9.3 The cone of learning (Dale, 1969). Personal elaboration.

This reality will also be more impactful by associating with another technology, AI. In the text "Life 3.0," Max Tegmark analyzes the impact of AI from different points of view. Still, the most bland and dangerous one could be using the same brightness. For this reason, the conscious and responsible use that especially companies will have to make and are making of it is essential: a controlled use and diffusion, so to speak, of the services and products that will be put on the market (Tegmark, 2018).

The applications of VR are different, one of which is to use it as a learning tool, from a technician repairing a photocopier to a worker needing to improve a high-definition power line.

Many real experiences can also be realistically experienced in a virtual environment. As Maxwell Maltz explains in the book *Psychocybernetics*, our minds do not distinguish between something experienced and vividly imagined (Maltz, 2016).

Here are some examples of where technology can be of help to humans:

■ use it as a feedback tool
■ provide remote assistance through simulations to decrease the risk of danger.

These procedures can be used as more effective learning processes, not only for purely specific and technical skills, also called "hard skills," but also regarding soft skills.

One possible thing in a virtual environment compared to a natural environment is manipulating objects and the damage or errors undone, thanks to a simple click. A different view of how to predict errors and limit risks to the business automatically results in money saved and, in extreme cases, even lives saved. Training in a virtual world has several advantages; for example, you can always reset everything if things go wrong. There are several examples in different fields; doctors have to deal with complex operations on children, thanks to simulation and 3D representation and the real nurse. In the military, pilots can use the room simulator, reducing costs and saving millions. Teachers can test a virtual classroom by challenging their courage in front of an unruly class, analyzing and testing disruptive behaviors.

As we understand, applying VR to different services can drastically cut costs, reduce expenses, and help many people improve their profession.

An example of a VR company is Impersive, which creates different experiences with a sense of immersion in the virtual world through 360°

perspective (stereoscopy, full-body, and motion). The full-body experience helps reduce motion sickness and disorientation by recognizing that users can participate in actions using the body. With 3D stereoscopy, one can see objects closer, as three-dimensional; due to this perception, there is more sense of reality and depth. With these tools, users can play and be the real protagonist, interacting with objects and other virtual humans. The application is extended to different fields: sports, automotive, education, entertainment, food, and industry.

For the police, training its employees using the VR model is more valuable than the traditional one. They use the Virtra system consisting of five 360° screens, and the room is set up with sound and vibration.

Walmart has more than 170 VR training academies in its system, and according to the company, "We want to find a way to train without interrupting operators." Ups has VR driver safety training in its programs. They realized the benefits of creating a unique skill by replicating locations and situations; this will reduce risk and problems on the job and increase the quality of services.

In addition, AR is a technology that allows the computer to generate virtual image information in the real world. VR can generate a virtual environment, but in AR, the environment is natural and is extended with information and images from the system (Lee, 2012).

According to several types of research conducted by Chang, Morreale, and Medicherla (2010), motivation in learning processes is higher when students use virtual and AR.

In education, especially in school, there are several advantages to studying subjects such as physics, chemistry, mathematics, biology, and astronomy, with the creation of augmented books allowing students to orient themselves. Becoming aware that all processes related to studying complex or tedious subjects will become more innovative and faster will increase students' understanding and motivation.

In business, AR is used in design processes and to recognize physical parts of products. Other applications are for cultural heritage in reconstructing ancient ruins and multimodal interaction techniques. For industries, it is possible to have practical assistance; for example, BMW is using this technology in production processes in the car repair and maintenance division. Museums use this system to display dinosaurs' real skeletons.

The future will be interactive education that will create a more interactive and enjoyable environment, and it will be possible to reduce costs in training and education (Lee, 2012).

As we have seen from the examples, VR is used and implemented to develop hard skills and knowledge. However, several researchers are considering using this technology to improve our soft skills. Anders Gronstedt, of the digital training consultancy known as the Gronstedt Group, said VR can take people into another world. However, users can also "walk a mile in another person's shoes." Of course, developing soft skills requires more thoughtfulness and creativity, but such a tool can teach empathy and basic skills to create a more inclusive and engaged workforce.

9.2 How the World of Training Is Changing

Let us start with a simple concept. When we talk about VR, we mean a combination of hardware and software to create a virtual space where the user can move. Thanks to VR viewers such as Oculus Quest 2, Quest 3, and Quest Pro, users can interact in new simulated realities, where eyes can perceive the surrounding space accurately, leading the user to "feel" like elsewhere.

What does this have to do with emotions? How can virtual and even AI help us get closer to reality? As we have just described, the viewers interact perfectly with our senses: sight, hearing, and touch. These psychological stimuli simulate actions, tricking and perceiving our minds as accurate. The actions we can perform in virtual environments are two: on the one hand, we can navigate, that is, move without restrictions; on the other hand, we can interact, for example, with objects. Our eyes are focused on the 3D and 360° experience, allowing the user to avoid external distractions. In addition, many viewers are also equipped with audio, so it is possible to insert headphones to keep hearing occupied. For this reason, a well-crafted experience with well-defined graphics and interaction can elicit emotions such as joy, happiness, or anxiety.

Another example of an innovative project is Vrainers, which has taken a step forward by incorporating AI, voice commands and generative AI, into VR. This means that not only are we able to see, hear, and interact with surrounding objects, but we can also communicate vocally with the environment or a virtual avatar (Vrainers, 2023).

9.2.1 Communication

One of the most in-demand soft skills on the market today is communication in many ways, not only as the art of speaking in front of a "real" audience and a "virtual" one. Let us consider how our working lives have changed during the "lockdown" period due to Covid-19. Companies have decided to have their employees work from home, which has led to the use of intelligent working; therefore, calls and constant meetings every day via Meet, Skype, Zoom, etc. Plus, for those who have chosen to launch their own online business, the ability to create high-value, short, concise videos has become the order of the day.

When you leave university, you realize that what you have done so far is just the tip of the iceberg and that the skills you have learned are not enough for the working world. So, what are companies looking for? Eighty-five percent of recruiters evaluate not only your technical skills but your ability to relate to others, how you fit in with people on a team, and how you "sell" yourself. A study conducted by Boston College, Harvard, and the University of Michigan shows that developing soft skills, such as communication and problem-solving, increases productivity by 12% and 250% on ROI, return on investment. LinkedIn found that the skills most in demand by recruiters are adaptability, collaboration, creativity, emotional intelligence, and persuasion. In the article by Ladders, "The seven skills that will matter the most in 2021," the analysis included active listening, adaptation, communication, emotional intelligence, innovation, teamwork, and work ethic.

So we can understand that the advent of new technologies is not at the gates but is already inside our homes!

The most trivial example can be the phone; let us think about the Alexa device; in particular, we are getting used to asking through its voice commands information on products, info about companies, listening to the radio or music, or buying a product.

So how do we relate to all this technological noise? As professionals, what can we focus on?

Given the premise of the entire book, the answer may have been guessed. In the book *AI for Dummies* by Massaron and Mueller, it is possible to analyze the seven types of intelligence. However, the most interesting aspect lies in the column "potential for comparison," which is how much a machine or AI can simulate the different types of intelligence (Table 7.1). The analysis shows that the lowest values correspond to interpersonal and intrapersonal intelligence; it is not a coincidence that we talk about introspection, interaction on different levels with others, or obtaining, exchanging, giving, and manipulating information.

Thanks to other studies conducted by experts and researchers, it has been possible to demonstrate what machines or AI cannot yet replicate. For this reason, we need not only to raise awareness of this critical aspect but also to understand what differentiates us when in our work, we hear, "We have invested in AI or new autonomous machines."

9.3 E-learning

E-learning (also known as "online training" or "distance learning") is a teaching method that uses digital technologies to deliver training and education courses at a distance. E-learning can deliver various courses, from vocational training courses to degree programs. It can be accessed through various devices like computers, tablets, and smartphones.

It offers several advantages over face-to-face learning, such as the flexibility for students to study at their convenience, access learning materials from anywhere, and study at their own pace. However, e-learning can also present challenges, such as a good internet connection and more direct interaction with teachers and classmates.

Moreover, the e-learning has become increasingly popular in recent years due to the Covid-19 pandemic, which forced many colleges and universities to close or restrict student access to school buildings. However, e-learning has been an alternative to face-to-face learning for many years.

9.3.1 Usefulness

There are many reasons why e-learning can be a good option for education or training.

- *Flexibility*: students can access course materials and complete lessons at their convenience without the constraints of in-person class schedules. This is especially useful for students who have work or family commitments.
- *Accessibility*: e-learning is accessible from anywhere with an internet connection, meaning students can study from anywhere.
- *Personalized learning pace*: students can study at their own pace without the pressure of keeping up with a group of classmates.
- *Costs*: e-learning is often more affordable than in-person instruction because there are no transportation or room and board expenses.

■ *Up-to-date instructional materials*: e-learning often uses digital instructional materials that can be easily updated and modified so that students can access up-to-date information.

However, it is essential to note that e-learning is only suitable for some students and can present challenges, such as the need for a good internet connection and more direct interaction with teachers and classmates.

9.3.2 Why Companies Use It

E-learning is a popular training tool for companies because it offers many advantages over in-person training. Here are some of the reasons why companies may choose to use e-learning for employee training:

■ *Flexibility*: employees can access the training material conveniently without taking leave or moving to a specific location. This is especially useful for companies with employees working in different locations or with family commitments.

■ *Saving time and money*: e-learning does not require employees to travel to a specific location for training, so companies can save time and money.

■ *Progress tracking*: e-learning platforms often offer tools to monitor employee progress and identify any areas of weakness that require further training.

■ *Up-to-date training materials*: As with education, e-learning for businesses often uses digital training materials that can be easily updated and modified, which means employees can access up-to-date information.

■ *Scalability*: e-learning can be easily scaled to train large groups of employees without holding in-person training events.

However, it is essential to note that e-learning is only suitable for some employees and may present challenges, such as the need for a good internet connection and the lack of direct interaction with teachers and classmates.

E-learning can be a valuable tool for human resources (HR) to provide training to employees and develop their skills. Here are some ways HR can use e-learning to support employee development:

- *Basic training*: HR can use e-learning to provide basic training on business processes, such as the performance management system or the hiring process.
- *Role-specific training*: e-learning can provide role-specific training, such as refresher courses on new software or work processes.
- *Soft skills development*: e-learning can be used to develop soft skills such as communication, problem-solving, or leadership.
- *Ongoing training*: HR can use e-learning to provide ongoing training to employees to maintain and develop their skills.
- *Progress tracking*: e-learning platforms often offer tools to monitor employee progress and identify any areas of weakness that require further training.

In addition, e-learning can be a valuable tool for HR to provide employees with efficient and low-cost training without organizing in-person training events. However, it is essential to note that it is only suitable for some employees and may present challenges, such as the need for a good internet connection and the lack of direct interaction with teachers and classmates.

9.3.3 Challenges

Video courses can present some challenges or disadvantages. Here are some of the main disadvantages of video courses:

- *Lack of interaction*: video courses may need more direct interaction with teachers or classmates, making it easier to get help or clarification on concepts needed help for understanding.
- *Dependence on technology*: video courses depend on the availability of technology, such as computers or mobile devices, which can be a challenge for some students.
- *Lack of motivation*: some students may need more human interaction to stay motivated to follow video courses.
- *Connection problems*: video courses often require a good internet connection, which can be problematic for those living in rural areas or with unstable internet connections.
- *Costs*: video courses can be more expensive than other training options, such as in-person courses or textbooks.

In general, video courses may be a good option for some people. However, it is essential to consider the possible disadvantages and assess whether they suit your learning needs.

9.3.4 On Working Days

Video courses can be a good option for work for several reasons. Here are some of the main ways video courses can be used in the world of work:

- *Employee training*: companies can use video courses to train their employees on specific topics, such as new technologies or safety practices.
- *Skills development*: video courses can develop employees' skills, such as providing foreign language or leadership courses.
- *Continuing education*: companies can use video courses to keep employees up-to-date on industry changes or new regulations and practices.
- *Distance learning*: video courses can be used to train employees who work in remote locations or cannot attend in-person courses.

In general, video courses can be a good option for companies looking to provide training and skill development to their employees efficiently and flexibly.

Here are some examples of how video courses can be used in the business world:

- A software company can use video courses to train its employees on a new development platform.
- A marketing company can use video courses to develop its employees' skills in social media marketing or data analytics.
- A logistics company can use video courses to keep its employees up-to-date on new regulations and practices related to workplace safety.
- A company with employees scattered across different regions can use video courses to provide distance learning on topics such as time management or interpersonal relationships.
- A university may use video courses to offer continuing education courses to its alums or to provide online degree programs to students who cannot attend in-person classes.

BOX 9.2: CASE STUDY—IMMERSED ON META QUEST STORE

An interesting app on the Meta Quest Store is Immersed, available for Oculus headsets. FOCUS on your work with massive screens in breathtaking virtual worlds! WORK with remote users in a virtual café! COLLABORATE with your team by sharing multiple screens or whiteboarding in person!

An interesting app that allows us to understand the world of work. Smart working and PCs are just the first step. Mixed reality will be the next.

References

Chang, G., Morreale, P., & Medicherla, P. (2010). Applications of augmented reality systems in education. In D. Gibson & B. Dodge (Eds.), *Proceedings of SITE 2010—Society for information technology & teacher education international conference* (pp. 1380–1385). San Diego, CA: Association for the Advancement of Computing in Education (AACE). Retrieved October 17, 2023 from https://www.learntechlib.org/primary/p/33549/.

Dale, E. (1969). Cone of learning. *Researchgate*. Available at: https://www.researchgate.net/figure/Cone-of-learning-by-Edgar-Dale-1969_fig1_265652174.

Hardy, D. (2022). *The compound effect.* London: John Murray Learning.

Lee, K. (2012). Augmented reality in education and training. *TechTrends*, 56(2), pp. 13–21. http://doi.org/10.1007/s11528-012-0559-3.

Maltz, M. (2016). *Psycho-cybernetics.* New York: TarcherPerigee, an imprint of Penguin Books.

Tegmark, M. (2018). *Life 3.0: Being human in the age of artificial intelligence.* Penguin Books.

Treccani. (n.d.). *APPRENDIMENTO in "Enciclopedia Italiana".* [online] Available at: https://www.treccani.it/enciclopedia/apprendimento_%28Enciclopedia-Italiana%29/.

Vrainers. (2023). Available at: https://vrainers.com/.

Chapter 10

Training and Coaching 3.0

10.1 What Does Training Mean?

The subject of training, a topical issue nowadays, has undergone significant methodological changes due to technological innovation, especially in the last two years due to the emergency we are still experiencing. Let us start with many people's questions: What does training mean? At first glance, this is a trivial question. Still, the answer refers to various concepts derived from different theories, which describe psychological processes we must deal with at every moment. Lucio Gallotti, a trainer and work psychologist, has stated that "training is a pathway, the objective of which is learning." In other words, it is a road to be traveled under the guidance of an experienced professional whose goal is acquiring new knowledge and skills. In the previous chapter, we already talked about learning, starting from the definition proposed by the psychologist Ernest Hilgard (1971), as *an intellectual process through which the individual acquires knowledge about the world that, subsequently, he uses to structure and orient his behavior in a lasting way.* Learning can result from spontaneous processes, as occurs in children, for example, with language, or it can be induced and guided through an external teaching intervention, a training course. Let us briefly discuss David Kolb's experiential learning theory, which is fundamental to teaching. The term experiential learning refers to two contrasting processes: on the one hand, it speaks of a pathway to the acquisition of new knowledge provided by external agents (institutions, professionals, and bodies): "direct experience with the phenomena studied rather than simply reflecting on the

                    DOI: 10.4324/9781003439691-13

experience, or merely consideration of the possibility of doing something about it" (Rubin, 1981).

On the other hand, much more simply, learning occurs spontaneously, so it is achieved through the reflection that each of us makes on everyday experience: "training that occurs as direct participation in the events of life" (Houle, 1980). Kolb, together with Roger Fry, identified a cyclical model of experiential learning consisting of four stages: concrete experience (emotional experience), reflective observation, abstract conceptualization (thinking), and active experimentation (action). According to experts, learning does not always start at the same point but can start at a different stage each time; this process often starts with a person taking action, which leads to consequences. The next step is to analyze that case to predict a given situation under the same circumstances. In other words, an individual who learns this way acquires rules of thumb or generalizations that enable him to predict and understand what to do in different situations. Do people think we have yet to discuss training in these last lines? The central role of the trainer is to maintain strong links between theory and practice. Kolb's model is closely linked to training because training is identified as a learning process based on experience. In addition, the trainer has learned from experience certain concepts and theoretical constructs that enable him to understand the characteristics of specific situations and then pass them on to others. There are different types of training, which very often depend on the different fields: training in companies for employees, managers or executives, or professionals; training in schools for students, parents, teachers, and principals; training in sports for athletes, parents, coaching staff, and sports managers; and behavioral training which is very often aimed at the personal sphere. Although the methodology changes depending on the target group and the field of application, the objective always remains to learn, and very often, the topics are the same; if we take, for example, the topic of communication, it is as important in school as in sport and work, as is the management of emotions.

10.2 Training 3.0

What is happening nowadays is a radical change in how training is done and the tools used. Why these transformations? On the one hand, continuous and fast technological innovation and, on the other hand, the experience of the last couple of years together have led to different and, each time, more complex needs and, at the same time, increasing pressures and demands. All this leads to the need for continuous training in all areas of our lives (work, sport, school, and personal sphere). Several possibilities have recently opened up for integrating classroom training with online training: an innovative, dynamic, and flexible way of training that only some people were used to four or five years ago. Today, however, it has become almost the norm, and the aim is to make more and more use of this new method called e-learning. Online training has many advantages: first, professionals can create lessons and interactive courses using different communication channels (video and audio). In addition, online training enables many people to be reached since events, teaching, and meetings can be followed anywhere in the world from the comfort of home without having to move. This system dramatically reduces costs for both the participants and, above all, the organizers.

The relevant aspect to focus on is the new frontiers that have been developing in recent years: training through VR. It has proved to be an excellent means of promoting learning, thanks to its adaptability since it can reproduce any virtual environment, allowing a dynamic approach to real problems. The first psychological studies and VR date back to the early 1990s, thanks to which we became aware of this technology's enormous potential in clinical psychology. It has been noted that virtual environments reproduced faithful to reality allow the subject under treatment to live a more precise experience than possible through imaginative capacity (Vincelli et al., 2006). Some examples of applications in psychology refer to the clinical field, specifically the treatment of phobias and post-traumatic stress disorder. In addition to these, more recently, VR seems to be an excellent means of enhancing learning: simulations in the military field, simulations of specific game situations for top-level sportsmen and women, simulations in the corporate field, and significantly improve specific skills (communication, management of emotions and conflict management) are becoming increasingly widespread. These new ways of training are much cheaper than traditional field training; the tasks are repeatable, constant monitoring, and carried out in entirely safe conditions. Look at other examples of the increasingly popular 3.0 training today.

The most common applications in this field concern the treatment of phobias. It is a marked fear or anxiety toward a specific object or situation. It involves intense anxiety with limited exposure to the presence of a particular stimulus, the phobic stimulus. Applications for treating phobias are based on "progressive exposure to the phobic stimulus and prevention of compulsive behavior" (DS). DS, developed by psychiatrist Joseph Wolpe (1972), aims to associate an antagonistic response to anxiety, such as muscle relaxation or controlled breathing, in the presence of the anxiety stimuli. In general, several studies have been conducted on treating several specific phobias, particularly fear of flying, agoraphobia, fear of driving, fear of spiders, and claustrophobia. VR environments can elicit the same emotions as the situation experienced in the real world and that the sense of presence can also be experienced in graphically inaccurate virtual environments. One of the specific phobias of our time is the fear of flying: 1 in 6 people are afraid of flying, avoiding taking the plane and thus feeding the resulting anxiety even more. When you are inside the plane, space is often minimal, and from the moment you leave until the moment you arrive, the only point of contact with the outside world is a small porthole. This situation can give rise to a fear of enclosed spaces (claustrophobia) in many people. An equal benefit for treating airplane phobia between VR and in-vivo exposure, with reduced costs and time due to treatment with virtual reality. Fear of driving, also known as amaxophobia, is widespread in Italy: 36% of men and 64% of women suffer from it. Also, in this case, many studies have confirmed the effectiveness of Virtual Reality Exposure Therapy (VRET): subjects with amaxophobia are exposed to anxiety-provoking situations in controlled conditions, allowing them to experience fear without being in a hazardous situation. This controlled exposure technique teaches subjects to manage their anxiety and maintain control. VR has also proved fundamental in treating the fear of spiders (arachnophobia), reducing time and costs compared to classical techniques (Gilroy et al., 2000). Studies on social phobia along the same lines have developed a protocol in VR structured around the four main situations recognized as threatening by subjects suffering from this disorder: requests for performance, situations of intimacy, judgment, and assertiveness. A phobia closely related to this one of social anxiety is the fear of speaking in public. Also, in this case, treatment of exposure through VR has led to surprising results, allowing users to experience themselves in virtual situations created ad hoc, such as class or work meetings (North et al., 1998). VR has also been shown to be effective in treating and preventing disorders other than anxiety in the clinical setting. For example, the use of VR in the treatment of OCD (obsessive compulsive disorder) involves vicarious exposure to stimuli related to contamination with the prevention of compulsive rituals (Clark et al., 1998). RV has also begun to complement the cognitive techniques used for eating disorders (DCA). Thanks to this technology, it is possible to construct specific virtual environments very similar to the real ones, characterized by anxiety-provoking and discriminating elements (supermarkets or restaurants). In this way, the individual can gradually learn to implement functional adaptive strategies in the virtual environment that can be easily transferred to the real context. RV training is also useful as a means of empowerment. One study that has demonstrated the effectiveness of VR in this field is that aimed at military training, as it is much cheaper than traditional field training, the tasks are repeatable, monitoring is constant, and it is carried out under completely safe conditions. These studies led to the development of flight simulators to support the training of aviation pilots, allowing them to improve their skills in a controlled manner. Today, this type of training is also used to empower certain skills, such as stress management. In cognitive enhancement, VR has become an important means of improving the athlete's tactical and mental skills. All these examples represent training methods because, as mentioned above, it involves a learning process. In these activities, from rehabilitation to mental training, the aim is to optimize certain behaviors by encouraging change and, thus, learning. It is important to remember that VR is an important means of prevention and learning. It allows one to live an experience directly, to "immerse" oneself in the concrete, virtually simulated situation. The content of this multisensory interface (involving sight and hearing but also movement) allows participants to live individualized and emotionally engaging experiences in a controlled context, learning from them and bringing them back to the real environment (transferability of learning).

10.3 Coaching

Once we have clarified what we are referring to when we talk about training, let us take a closer look at its specific practical applications. Today, we will talk about a training methodology that has become increasingly popular in different areas of our lives and is undergoing profound changes with the development of new technologies: coaching. Coaching is a methodology based on an equal relationship between coach and client, which aims to develop, train, and acquire valuable strategies and techniques to achieve specific goals in the future. It should be emphasized that it is not a way to alleviate mental or emotional pain/trauma; instead, this is not its purpose; in fact, it is a methodology based on active learning that does not include a psychodiagnostic approach. In other words, coaching is an effective tool for enhancing one's performance at work, in sports, or in the personal sphere: a path of individualized personal growth where the watchword is "change." Let us take a closer look at the different application areas of this methodology. Concerning the personal sphere, we speak of *Life Coaching*, a path co-constructed by the professional and the client, aimed at the person's future. As mentioned, this work aims not to reduce pain or manage psychological discomfort but to achieve goals for the individual to enhance performance. The life coach makes his or her knowledge, strategies, and personal experience available, acting as a non-intrusive guide without imposing himself or herself but basing the whole process on a "let us proceed together" relationship. In this way, people can clarify and pursue their goals, improve communication and relationships, enhance organizational skills, and increase their work-life balance. As far as the world of work is concerned, such a path is identified with *Business Coaching*. In this case, the intervention is intended for managers, executives, professionals, entrepreneurs, employees, and anyone interested in addressing professional and corporate issues. Business coaching is a methodology for developing personal resources to enhance work performance and productivity, increase self-efficacy levels, improve communication and professional relations, and strengthen the ability to choose and delegate. Therefore, thanks to personal resources, anyone undertaking such a path can achieve challenging and concrete objectives within their operational context. Coaching can also be applied in sports to guide athletes to rediscover their resources and acquire new skills. In this case, the protagonist of the process is the athlete. However, the technical staff (coaches and managers) and the intervention aim to facilitate the identification of concrete objectives, increase motivation, and ensure effective management of the post-match, all aspects that aim to enhance performance. Coaching is, therefore, a process aimed at developing personal resources based on a one-to-one relationship, which does not involve the use of psychodiagnostic tools or techniques and the management of psychological discomfort or problems of a pathological nature. Another aspect I would like to highlight is the willingness of the individual to start such an intervention because, as we said at the beginning, change is the final result of coaching. There must be a direct and conscious request from the person, with a clear intention to get involved. Otherwise, the effectiveness of the process will always be low.

10.3.1 Changes with Web 3.0

Before talking about the changes that have taken place in this field, let us try to set the context in which and during which they took place. Since 2010, there has been talk of a change of course with the advent of Web 3.0: in technical terms, this term refers to a set of emerging technologies developed by large companies such as Google or IBM, by small companies dedicated to developing this type of content, such as Radar Networks, and by the valuable contribution of various researchers and developers around the world. In practical terms, with this new vision, we see a concentration of multiple layers of meaning, managed and processed by systems that use the human reasoning process. We talk about the "Semantic Web," a term introduced by the British computer scientist Tim Berners-Lee to indicate the transformation of the internet into an environment in which online data, or rather metadata, are associated with information that can be interpreted and is suitable for automatic processing. If we tried to explain what has just been said, we could say that Web 3.0 uses AI technology, thanks to which, interacting with humans, it automatically processes a set of information and makes it immediately available as if it were a web page. At this point, more and more in-depth and evolved searches will be possible based on links of information and documents carried out in an elaborate, logical, and automatic way. This will undoubtedly change our ways of communicating and interacting with new technologies, especially considering the period we have lived in these last two years worldwide. In addition, methodologies and techniques are undergoing several changes to adapt and keep up with technological innovation.

Coaching has undergone profound changes due to the emergency period we live in today, forcing us to use other types of tools that have limited face-to-face training. All these elements have led to the increasing diffusion of online or mixed coaching, which often creates difficulties for the coach, especially the client. On the other hand, they have stimulated us to give space to our creative abilities and the increasing use of innovative tools such as VR. VR is now becoming part of these resource development paths in all the areas described here. We need only refer to the numerous applications in the field of sport, starting with simulations of specific game situations through VR settings (tennis) or repetitions of racecourses (motor racing, skiing, etc.). Also, in the world of work, for example, the Vrainers team has created an efficient training program that helps people work on themselves and then train their communication skills, aiming to optimize the "art of public speaking." Today, many companies are investing in this direction; Vrainers, for example, believes strongly in this technology, which, together with AI systems, has a high potential in the context of performance enhancement: they are, in fact, innovative means that can facilitate the degree of involvement of people through their concrete and practical approach, thus increasing personal motivation. The protagonist of all projects, interventions, and paths Vrainers creates is always the individual, to improve his or her quality of life and psychological well-being.

10.4 Soft Skills

Today, due to the speed at which the market and technologies evolve, companies no longer consider only capable and technically competent people but also their ability to adapt to change, the way they express themselves, their ability to work in a team, and even their level of leadership (Serby, 2003). According to research, 15% of business requirements are hard skills, and 85% are soft skills (Watts & Watts, 2008).

In 2012, a survey conducted by Tracker and Yost evaluated several students in teams, realizing that to achieve desired results, students need training to perform. To develop these skills or traits, people need specialized training and courses.

According to the National Employer Skills Survey (2003), a person unable to communicate correctly is likelier to create a negative impression than someone with lower skills but more excellent communication skills. The goal of training is to remove blocks and barriers that are helpful for students who want to look for new jobs and employees.

As shown in the study conducted by Schulz, soft skills are just as critical as academic knowledge and highlighting the fact that educators complained about students because of the lack of soft skills such as teamwork, communication skills, and today not having specific skills puts you at a disadvantage compared to others (Schulz, 2008).

According to the study, to meet the needs of the European market made by Andrews and Higson, the education of students must contain not only knowledge and skills but also skills that go beyond. Employability focuses on adapting to a new environment, working in companies with different cultures and flexibility. The study was done in four countries: the United Kingdom, Austria, Slovenia, and Romania (Andrews & Higson, 2010), establishing the 11 most relevant skills: professionalism, reliability, ability to cope with uncertainty, ability to work under pressure, ability to communicate and interact with others, written and verbal communication skills, information and communication technology skills, creativity and self-confidence, good time management and self-management, and willingness to learn and accept responsibility.

In addition, the study found three main themes that are relevant and in line with market demands:

■ technical or known as "hard" skills;
■ interpersonal skills: soft skills;
■ work experience and work-based learning.

As we can see, it shows again that the combination of hard and soft is inevitable. Another relevant aspect emerged from the interviews with students, asking about their views on their degrees and thoughts. However, employees' views are also based on softer skills such as communication, presentation, innovative thinking, and people who can express fresh ideas and think outside the box, which is a highly valued skill.

At the end of the study, the central concept that emerged was related to the synergistic complication of tangible and intangible skills and problem-solving ability; the mix of hard skills, soft skills, and work experience background is what they referred to as "employment-ready," and as a result, in-house training will be more accessible (Andrews & Higson, 2010).

Further research has been done with the support of the University of Chicago on how soft skills can predict success in life by measuring cognitive skills. Tests and grades have always judged our intelligence or mental abilities; however, success in life also depends on personality traits that influence behavior, such as conscientiousness, perseverance, sociability, and curiosity.

The terms ability and character suggest that it can be improved and learned. In the past, France's minister of public education introduced the first tool to measure intelligence to understand students' futures. Alfred Binet created the IQ test. In addition, they developed a standardized achievement test. Many psychologists do not recognize IQ, where performance tests and grades are a way to measure cognitive ability and intelligence.

Psychological traits are manifest thoughts, feelings, behaviors, and performance on tasks, and it is possible to develop them through practices, investments of time, money, and habits. As a result of the research, five skills known as the "Big Five" were considered: openness to experience, conscientiousness, extroversion, agreeableness, and neuroticism. The only problem is that it is difficult to measure these skills; in Robert's definition of personality, all psychological measurement is influenced by incentives and other traits. There are two aspects behind the behavior: the first depends on the incentives created in the different situations, and the second depends on more traits.

The results of the report conclude that according to the studies of personality traits, it is possible to predict and cause the outcomes, which could be measured by performing tasks. In addition, cognitive ability is essential for tasks of higher complexity. For the authors, the most important innovation that could be made in this field is to promote a beneficial change in personality to foster human development.

In a 2010 study by Klaus, ten soft skills were identified: integrity, communication, courtesy, responsibility, social skills, positive attitude, professionalism, flexibility, teamwork, and work ethic. However, technology significantly impacts our lives and skill development (Mitchell et al., 2010).

In the beginning, companies required only technical skills, but today, according to the study, 25% is technical knowledge and 75% is human skills for long-term job success (Klaus, 2010). A questionnaire was done, and 91 students were selected and asked what importance they placed on the ten selected skills. From the study, it was found that communication was the most important to the students. In addition, to describe the meaning of soft skills, we can think of something that does not have technical, intangible, personality-specific skills (such as leader, facilitator, mediator, and negotiator) and the combination of interpersonal skills and personal attributes. Companies that have workers with such skills could provide a competitive advantage, and some companies decide to devote part of their budget to resource training, knowing that the investment will bring a return. There are also several implications for corporate educators, having the ability to understand the level of success based on what is known and how it is communicated.

In conclusion, it can be understood that soft skills are an investment, and companies and individuals should be aware of this (Robles, 2012).

Going back to what was analyzed in the table of intelligence, soft skills are considered interpersonal and relational skills, something that today an artificial system is not yet able to replicate; a short consideration if we want to find something in which, as humans, we must invest.

10.4.1 The Benefits of Soft Skills in the Digital Era

Today's job market is becoming more competitive than it was 30 or 40 years ago, whereas, in the post-war era, labor market demand exceeded the number of people looking for work. Back then, finding a job was more accessible, and the only thing that mattered was related to skills and knowledge. However, today the situation is entirely different, the competition for a job is higher, and the demand for jobs is different. Companies prefer more productive candidates who can, in a job interview, show skills such as courtesy, honesty, and flexibility (Schulz, 2008). An example would be knowledge of body language, which allows you to cover up feelings of uncertainty and insecurity.

Nowadays, people can acquire these skills in different ways. Due to the information age, people can acquire information from a simple PC and Wi-Fi connection. According to Schulz, there are at least three different methods to get it:

- *Formal training*: people who want to implement and develop soft skills can attend training classes and choose courses in rhetoric, languages, presentations, and public speaking;
- *Self-education*: by reading books (now also possible by listening to podcasts and through video courses);
- *Digital learning*: based on using the new technology known as e-learning.

All of them could yield superior results than using only one (Schulz, 2008). It is necessary to find a balance between them. They are also related to the technologies we know and can use. Thinking about electronic learning, some years ago, it was not possible.

According to the "Future of Jobs" report by the World Economic Forum, LinkedIn conducted an analysis describing that in 2019, soft skills were more in demand to obtain employment. In the report, human skills will increase in value as technology and automation advance. Furthermore, as LinkedIn's director of learning, Paul Pedrone, wrote, "Soft skills will be the best investment you can make in your career."

Furthermore, we are deep into the fourth industrial revolution, and humans need skills. Due to the increasing instability and the continuous change of job profiles, employees must be more flexible and retrain periodically, as shown in Figure 10.1 from the World Economic Forum and the Future of Jobs Survey of 2023.

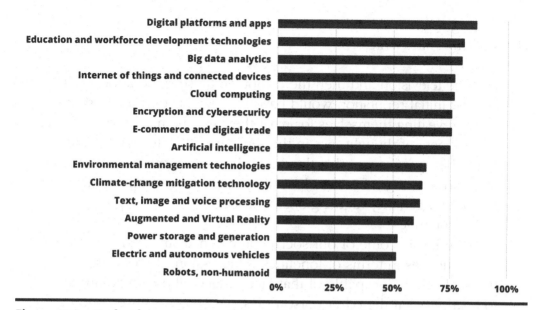

Figure 10.1   Technology adoption, 2023–2027. Personal elaboration.

As the figure indicates, it is visible that the percentage is increasing, where critical thinking and analysis, problem-solving, and self-management about personal and interpersonal skills prevail. While concerning "hard skills" data, "Technology use and development" prevails.

With Table 10.1, taken from the report published by the World Economic Forum in 2020, it is possible to analyze the 15 most in-demand skills for 2025.

Learning soft skills will be an advantage to succeed and stay competitive with the advent of intelligent machines. Why do we need to consider soft skills and the digital world? The advent and rise of unemployment, AI, and VR are what we need to develop and train.

Table 10.1   Top Industries for Increasing Skills Requirements, 2023–2027

1	Cognitive skills
2	Engagement skills
3	Technology skills
4	Physical abilities
5	Management skills
6	Self-efficacy, working with others, and ethics

To also give some thought to the topic, Galimberti, within the book *The Myths of Our Time*, writes.

> First the television and then the computer, these "kind appliances," as their initial reputation would have it, today have thrown off the mask, revealing themselves for what they are: the most formidable conditioners of thought, not in the sense that they tell us what to think, but in the sense that they radically modify our way of thinking, transforming it from analytical, structured, sequential and referential, into generic, vague, global, holistic.
>
> He continues,
>
> What has become of our social competence, and what are the consequences in terms of loneliness, depression, shyness, for having become incapable of that face-to-face where, in addition to hearing what the other person says, we perceive his emotional movements, the quality of his feelings, and in general all that language that does not pass through the word but the body, and that is essential for the formation of an identity which, like the strength of character, confidence, determination, perseverance, is not downloaded from a website?

10.4.2 Developing Soft Skills with VR and AI

In the 21st century, social-emotional skills are the most critical and relevant skills. Individuals with solid and soft skills can be effective collaborators, leaders, and good citizens.

Thinking about how the training scenario is developing, there are so many critical aspects that in the past, it was impossible to find a solution due to time and resources, and traditional learning methods were related to live courses, video courses, and videos in general, or books. However, thanks to the advent of new technologies, tracking a person's behavior in real time and giving feedback simultaneously will be possible. If the action performed has a positive response, the software will try to gratify the correct behavior instead of punishing it.

By analyzing the human brain, we can find two distinct learning systems: cognitive skills, related to "what," characterized by passive observations, study, and metallic repetition; and behavioral skills, related to "how," which means empathy, embracing diversity such as eye contact, and being respectful. Learning processes are more related to "doing processes," psychological repetition, and emotional processes that help understand on a visceral level and target harassment, bias, and prejudice. For example, in commercial sectors, there is an opportunity to train employees with more relevant and compelling qualities to increase customer satisfaction.

In this situation, a learner who does not respond correctly and has poor soft skills will receive negative feedback due to total immersion in the situation and the feeling of presence. The perfect combination of realistic interpersonal reactions and real-time communication can increase empathy and help understand and embrace diversity.

Most applications between AR/VR and AI are conducted on gaming and entertainment or training and situation simulation.

Due to the requirements for using these technologies, companies and trainers will have a great deal of information regarding their customers. As a result, the more information there is, the greater the possibility of making predictions and targeting the right customer.

VR is capable of modeling physics, motion, and material interactions. In addition, the combination of VR and AI is disruptive, unlocks more confidence and competence for the intelligent machine, and can create a self-training system. The next step will be VR and boot camp and how to match these dimensions and all these technologies together.

We understand that VR is computer-generated, and it is an entirely artificial environment where people can learn within a fully immersive environment. Users can move around, hear sounds, and interact with their surroundings. Thanks to the smartphone, it works with the PlayStation (Oculus Rift) or through the same app. According to research on Responsive Virtual Human (RVH) technology, using an intelligent agent that combines VR with natural language processing could be a disruptive innovation. Indeed, RVH can replicate emotional, psychological aspects, and cognitive states. Advantages include increased classroom training and the fact that learning can be transferred more efficiently; in other words, there is an opportunity to gain more hands-on experience with greater confidence supported by the virtual environment. If there is an opportunity to implement VR and natural languages, people can practice public speaking, communication, and negotiation skills.

VR is useful for exploring a fully immersive computer-generated world. The most relevant trends are:

■ AR and VR with IA;
■ VR and AR for training and teaching;
■ entertainment and mainstream;
■ collaboration and socializing.

Starting with the former, AI with machine learning algorithms can increase intelligence next year by including voice control in VR; for example, players will have more opportunities for challenges in video games. VR can reduce risks and costs for training and teaching, especially for surgery. Walmart is already increasing its program by training its employees with VR, and the U.S. military is dealing with Microsoft and their new Hololens product, having as goals: developing route finding, target acquisition, and mission planning.

To summarize this part, VR and VR will take place, and the combination of them with AI will be the new disruptive technology and all the possible applications in different fields. One example is the possibility of using these technologies to improve people's skills and to develop programs that can help coaches, trainers, or psychologists produce specific programs for their clients.

References

Andrews, J., & Higson, H. (2010). *Graduate employability, "soft skills" versus "hard." business knowledge: A European study* (pp. 411–422). [ebook]. Available at: https://www.tandfonline.com/doi/abs/10.1080/03797720802522627.

Clark, A. et al. (1998). A pilot study of computer-aided vicarious exposure for obsessive-compulsive disorders. *Australian and New Zealand Journal of Psychiatry*, 32, 268–275.

Gilroy, L.J. et al. (2000). Controlled comparison of computer-aided vicarious exposure versus live exposure in the treatment of spider phobia. *Behavior Therapy*, 31(4), 733–744.

Hilgard, E., & Bower, G. (1971). *Le teorie dell'apprendimento*. Milan: Angeli.

Houle, C.O. (1980). *Continuing learning in the professions*. San Francisco: Jossey-Bass.

Klaus, P. (2010). Communication breakdown. *California Job Journal*, 28, 1–9.

Mitchell, G.W., Skinner, L.B., & White, B.J. (2010). Essential soft skills for success in the twenty-first century workforce as perceived by business educators. *Delta Pi Epsilon Journal*, 52, 43–53.

North, M.M. et al. (1998). Virtual reality therapy: An effective treatment for the fear of public speaking. *International Journal of Virtual Reality*, 3(3), 1–6.

Robles, M. (2012). *Executive perception of the top 10 soft skills needed in today's workplace*. [ebook] SAGE. Available at: https://www.researchgate.net/profile/Marcel_Robles/publication/258126575_Executive_Perceptions_of_the_Top_10_Soft_Skills_Needed_in_Today's_Workplace/links/560 95e8908ae4d86bb11d036/Executive-Perceptions-of-the-Top-10-Soft-Skills-Needed- in-Todays-Workplace.pdf.

Rubin, L.B. (1981). *Field study: A sourcebook for experimental learning.* AbeBooks. Available at: https://www.abebooks.com/9780803900509/Field-Study -Sourcebook-Experimental-Learning-0803900503/plp.

Serby, R. (2003). Importance of Soft Skills. Available at: http:// .www.directionsmag .com/article.php?article_id=418.

Schulz, B. (2008). *The importance of soft skills: Education beyond academic knowl- edge.* [ebook] NAWA – Journal of Language and Communication. Available at: http://ir.nust.na/bitstream/handle/10628/39/The%20Importance%20of%20Soft %20%2 0Skills-Education%20beyond%20academic%20knowledge.pdf?sequence =1&isAllowed=y.

Vincelli, F., Molinari, E.E., & Riva, G. (2006). *La realtà virtuale in psicologia clinica: Nuovi percorsi di intervento nel disturbo di panico con agorafobia.* Milan: McGraw-Hill.

Watts, M., & Watts, R.K. (2008). Developing soft skills in students. Available at: http://l08.cgpublisher.com/proposals/64/index_html.

Wolpe, J. (1972). Review of *Behavior Therapy and Beyond* [Review of the book *Behavior Therapy and Beyond*, by A. A. Lazarus]. *Professional Psychology, 3*(4), 390–392.

Chapter 11

About World 3.0

11.1 Communication

Deciding to embark on a pathway dedicated to oneself can also involve communication-related work. This is a concept that has evolved a great deal over the years, allowing people to adapt to different situations; just consider, for example, the last two years in which the Covid emergency has led to a considerable reduction in personal relationships, in contact with friends and relatives and, on the other hand, has led to an exponential spread of intelligent working. We talk about communication as if it were easy and intuitive to understand what we are talking about. Still, it is a very complex process involving many problematic psychological and social functions. There are different definitions of this process. Let us look at something specific about this and then focus on the new frontiers proposed by today's technologies.

One of the most critical scholars is Anolli, whose studies have attempted to identify the main characteristics of communication. According to him, communication is simultaneously a social, cognitive, action-related, and participatory activity: "Communication is an observable interactive exchange between two or more participants, endowed with mutual intentionality and a certain level of awareness" (Anolli et al., 2003). Interpreting the message between the two interlocutors becomes essential within the communicative process. This is referred to as intention-in-action (Anolli et al., 2001), according to which the effectiveness of the interaction depends on the meaning derived from the reciprocal interpretation at an intentional level. After

DOI: 10.4324/9781003439691-14

several types of research (Airenti et al., 1993; Anolli et al., 2002; Anolli & Mantovani, 2011), a univocal definition of the communicative process has been arrived at: "a process of co-construction of meaning that takes place in the here and now of the conversation and in which the speaker and his interlocutors are co-actors."

11.1.1 Communicating through Technology

As already mentioned, technology is composed of "mediums," means of communication that allow subjects to overcome the constraints of face-to-face interaction. The changes due to the continuous technological evolution have aroused increasing interest in psychology to understand the characteristics and effects of the new media on individual behavior. In particular, it has focused on the relationship between these tools and how they communicate. Indeed, as I have already stated, our communication processes are increasingly influenced by these new media. What is lacking in the study of new mediums is a theoretical approach capable of describing the dynamics of mediated communication within human activity. In fact, due to the complexity of the subject, psychologists have increasingly devoted themselves to the applied rather than the theoretical aspect. An important and emerging role in this field is entrusted to the psychology of new media, also called "cyberpsychology." This area of psychology is characterized by its multidisciplinary nature, combining knowledge from cognitive psychology, sociology, communication psychology, and ergonomics. The main objective of new media psychology is "the study, understanding, prediction, and activation of change processes that have their main origin in interaction with new media." In this sense, we speak of *communication mediated by new media*, which we will refer to with the abbreviation of *mediated communication*, as that "form of communication between two people through a technological instrument, which carries out a digital processing of information" (Riva, 2012). Anolli states that "each subject chooses whether or not to be a communicator, but he or she can choose whether and how to communicate" (Anolli, 2002). In this sense, the media represent mediating devices, facilitating communication through an indirect (mediated) perception of the other.

How, then, can technology help us? Generally speaking, it has enabled us to maintain relations with family and friends and continue certain work activities in a critical situation such as the one we have been experiencing for two years. In communication, I would like to focus on virtual reality. Virtual reality, in the context of the relationship, can be used as an instrument of "shared" communication (Riva & Davide, 2001): "Virtual reality can be considered as a three-dimensional and interactive extension of traditional graphic chats." In this sense, action has also been taken in the recreational sphere by creating video games for PC, which allow a high level of interactivity for the user and the possibility of creating instant chats during use. Amusement parks worldwide are also gradually introducing interactive virtual reality platforms, conveying unique and highly engaging experiences. Let us now analyze the critical aspects on which the new technologies are based.

One of the first aspects of new media is *content*. The gradual digitization has led to the "possibility of consulting and manipulating the same content regardless of the technology used" (Riva, 2010).

This technological evolution has done nothing but produce new opportunities leading to two consequences concerning contents and fruition (Tessarolo, 2007):

■ *Content dematerialization*: content is no longer connected to a physical object.
■ *Disintegration*: the user becomes a "spectacle-author" by creating and editing content (Pulcini, 2006) and a "comment-author" by discussing and sharing content (Riva, 2007).

A concept closely linked to that of new media, defined as mediating devices, is that of "change." There has been a great deal of research that has sought to understand the impact of this process of technological digitization. Shannon and Weaver (1949) state that a medium influences the communicative activity of the users who interact with it at three levels: physical (through the natural characteristics of the medium), symbolic (through the signifiers needed to interact with the media device), and pragmatic (through the set of actions with which the user uses the medium). It has also been observed that "the medium interacts with the social and individual structure in a continuous feedback relationship" (Watzlawick, 1976). This statement explains that the media's characteristics can influence its user's behavior and, in the same way, attitudes and new trends can modify the medium itself.

A practical example is the SMS message, which cannot exceed 160 characters. First of all, the user must therefore know the characteristics of the medium to avoid misunderstandings in the communication (short message interpreted as a desire to close the discussion). This limitation of the number of characters leads the individual to invent new means to overcome this constraint (abbreviations or icons representing emotional states). On the other hand, the increasing use of SMS has also changed the structure of the medium with a more complete keyboard that makes the writing process easy. Another change introduced by the new media is that of the role of the body in interaction. While in the face-to-face communicative exchange, the subject is the body, with the introduction of mediums, the subject becomes "disembodied" for his interlocutor. A virtual body replaces real bodily physicality. The first consequence of this change is that the issue can no longer use the other's body to understand their emotions. Moreover, the message is the subject itself, but it separates from it, acquiring its autonomy and stability over time. In today's rapidly changing context, the medium is considered an *artifact*, defined as "any object used by humans in their activity to coordinate themselves in the physical and social environment" (Cole & Engestrom, 1993).

"An artifact is an aspect of the material world modified by its history of inclusion within a goal-directed activity" (Cole, 1996). According to this view, the subject is defined as an "actor" who engages in behavior influenced and mediated by artifacts to satisfy needs/intentions. This fulfillment depends on the perceived abilities of the subject (skills) and the opportunities seized through artifacts deriving from the environment and culture (challenge). This last aspect introduces another fundamental concept, *affordance*, defined as "a resource that the environment offers to a subject capable of grasping it" (Gibson, 1979). Every object or environment has physical properties that suggest particular actions and not others. The subject, guided by their intentions, has a wide choice of different properties of the artifact helpful in achieving the purpose. The level of usefulness depends not only on the meaning but also on the situation, referring to it as "the information system that contains all the information about the delimited part of the environment in which the action takes place, including social information" (Matovani, 1996). This affordance differs on two levels:

- *Direct affordance*: direct influence resulting from a flow of information the environment provides. In this case, it is the physical characteristics of an object or environment.
- *Mediated affordance*: the result of an interpretation by the subject regarding the situation or object/environment. This refers to the meaning attributed to the object and the context in which the individual is placed.In this perspective, affordance is an *opportunity for action* or *inhibition provided by the situation to the individual*. One factor that provides a medium opportunity for mobilization is the intention, which plays a fundamental role in guiding the subject's action.

They are diverse and can be categorized on three levels which, according to *the dynamic theory of intentions* (Pacherie, 2006), use different information processing systems:

1. *Distal intentions*: these are those oriented toward the future, based on the rational cognitive system, system 2, referred to by Kahneman (2002), guided by awareness, reflection, and reasoning, but at the same time, very wasteful and slow.
2. Proximal intentions are oriented toward the present, based on both the intuitive and rational cognitive systems, depending on the subject's skills. The individual will use the fastest system (transparent artifact) since there is no longer a need to refer to reasoning and action planning. Beginners need the more reflective system 2 (opaque relic).
3. *Motor intentions*: those of enacting the action itself, based on the intuitive system, *system 1*, which generates quick and low expenditure impressions but is not voluntary, reasoned, and conscious (Kahneman, 2002).

Therefore, the user's activity is articulated on three levels, including managing the lower ones. A further aspect to which it is essential to refer, starting from the definition of medium, is "mediated action," the need for tools (artifacts) necessary to achieve a goal. There are two types of mediated action: *direct* and *indirect*. In the first case, the subject has direct control over the artifact to achieve the intention in the context in which it is located through the movement of the body: in the case of a tennis player using the racket (proximal artifact) to hit the ball (intention) or in the case of a media, the sliding of the finger on the smartphone (motor intention) to read an SMS (proximal intent). In the second case, the subject, through body movement, controls an artifact with which it manages other artifacts to satisfy the intention in the environment.

An example of this kind is the video game, in which the user moves a joystick (proximal artifact) with his hand with which to control an avatar (proximal artifact) to kick a ball (intention). The first aspect that distinguishes these two modes of action is the complexity, which is greater in the second case. Moreover, another factor that differentiates them and introduces us to a key concept of new media is *the effect they have on our experience, which is different*: direct mediated actions lead to the *incorporation of the artifact*, while indirect mediated actions lead to *the embodiment of the artifact*. "The effective use of an artifact extends the peripersonal space". Let us return to the example of the tennis player who hits the ball with the racket's movement. If the player becomes an expert and uses the artifact intuitively, perceptual incorporation of the artifact is produced. In other words, the racket becomes an extension of the arm (the proximal artifact becomes present in us). The racket goes from opaque to transparent at a perceptual level about the subject's intentions. Regarding the effect of indirectly mediated actions, the studies started in the early 1990s on teleoperations have made a significant contribution. These are tasks carried out by a robot (teleoperator) controlled at a distance by the perceptive and motor skills of a human operator (Riva, 2000). These studies, together with the development of virtual reality, have made it possible to explain a fundamental concept that characterizes the new media: presence, defined as "the sensation of being in an environment, real or virtual, resulting from the ability to intuitively put one's intentions into action in the environment, also through the artifacts it contains" (Riva, 2007). Already with the study of teleoperation, human operators, once they had become experts, reported feeling "present" (telepresence) in the remote environment in which the teleoperator was located. With virtual reality, moreover, it has been concluded that it is possible to experience a "sense of presence" even within a simulated environment. "The subject becomes, therefore, present in a virtual body" (Lenggenhager et al., 2007). One can summarize what has been said so far with the following statement: a new medium becomes an affordance, an opportunity for its users when it can implement its intentions (presence) and understand those of others (social presence). These are the foundations for a medium to become an opportunity for action not an inhibition for the subject. The future of the new media is thus oriented toward inter-reality, a continuous exchange of mutual influence between the real and virtual dimensions. If we try to update what has been said so far, we only have to think of the emergency period we lived through because of Covid-19. On 20 March 2020, the World Health Organization (WHO) declared a pandemic status due to Covid-19. In July 2021, more than 14 million cases were reported and around 600,000 deaths worldwide, a figure that passed the one million mark in September. Health measures during this period focused on hygiene practices, such as frequent hand washing, mask-wearing, and social distancing, all aimed to limit the spread of the virus. The direct consequence of these measures was the interruption of medical services, medical examinations, and non-urgent interventions, even for fragile and vulnerable people, creating long waiting lists and appointments postponed for a year or two. In this context, the introduction of telecommunication tools in hospitals has made it possible to maintain a doctor-patient relationship. Specifically, virtual reality has proved to be excellent support in health monitoring and rehabilitation. One can speak, therefore, of telemedicine or, even more recently, "e-Health," a term that, according to the WHO, describes the use of technologies linked to information and telecommunications, known as ICT (Information and Communication Technologies) to generate a beneficial effect on the health of citizens. Today, smartphones, tablets, and virtual reality have been incorporated into hospitals, allowing visits and treatments to be carried out remotely. Several studies have demonstrated virtual reality's effectiveness in treating multiple sclerosis, allowing continuous communication outside hospital facilities. In addition, interventions of this kind have proved effective for chronic neurological patients and those with cognitive impairment, where virtual reality makes it possible to maintain a high level of involvement in these patients while at the same time enhancing it in prolonged interventions at home. Again, this innovative technology has proven effective in cognitive behavioral interventions for patients with eating disorders and as a tool for empowering visual-spatial skills in people with unilateral spatial neglect. Finally, virtual reality has also been used in surgical interventions to limit exposure to possible infections and optimize precision. As we can see, new technologies have been beneficial in maintaining an active and effective communication channel during the pandemic.

11.1.2 The Art of Public Speaking

Public speaking is not innate and can be trained and optimized through various exercises. This ability includes good management of emotions and creating good relationships with others through effective verbal and nonverbal communication. First of all, however, it is essential to work on ourselves because if we have a good relationship with ourselves (self-esteem, sincerity), we can also relate to others without any particular difficulty. Seneca taught us: "Learn to like yourself. What you think of yourself is much more important than what others think. But you may wonder what it means to work on yourself and how you can do it."

Each of us has skills, behaviors, and thinking styles that characterize our being in the world. Some skills are innate and part of our genetic makeup, while others are learned through life-long experiences. When we talk about personal work, we mean a structured path of guidance and support for the individual to strengthen some effects that characterize the person. It is real training, as it happens in sports, which requires perseverance, commitment, and willpower, in which the individual can be considered the athlete and the psychologist the coach. Let us take communication as an example: it is a process of information exchange between two or more people in a specific context. There are two main ways of doing this: words and signals from our bodies. The former is called verbal communication, which includes spoken and written language. At the same time, the latter is identified as nonverbal communication, which refers to silent language (clothing, body gestures, and facial expressions). Several theories consider language as an innate ability (Chomsky, 1986) and others, instead, as abilities learned through experience (Skinner, 1957), but I am not here to give you a theoretical lecture. It is essential, however, to know that within a communicative exchange, it is not only the sharing of the same linguistic code that counts but also the meaning attributed to the message transmitted. For example, a humorous joke can include the intention to make the other person laugh, be noticed, or seduce them. In this regard, the paralinguistic system comes into play, including nonverbal communication, that is, the tone and timbre of the voice and the rhythm of the speech, which can facilitate the attribution of the right intention linked to the message transmitted. But let us return to our specific case: public speaking. As already mentioned above, the ability to speak in public can be trained. First, it is essential to enhance individual aspects of the person, starting with self-confidence, accepting one's limits, and leveraging strengths to improve oneself. In this context, emotions play a relevant role: recognizing them, getting them for what they are, and managing them optimally is a good prerequisite for a successful speech. Feeling produces changes in breathing and speech articulation, which in turn partly determine the parameters of the acoustic signal. In other words, fear can cause a low voice, difficulty in understanding, and restricted body language, all signs that, in the eyes of the listener, can be interpreted as insecurity on the speaker's part. Therefore, finding ways to effectively regulate one's emotions (increase or decrease emotional states) is fundamental for a successful speech and all other life contexts.

A personal course can be fundamental to optimize or prevent a frequent problem in this field: fear of public speaking. In psychology, this type of problem is often encountered, characterized by a strong feeling of anxiety at the mere thought of having to give a speech in front of a group of people. This situation is a source of stress for many people and, in some cases, can reach high levels of stress, leading to psychological problems. Classical therapy usually involves gradual exposure to the stimulus (cognitive behavioral therapy), combined with social skill training and relaxation techniques. It is never easy for a person to go through such a process because the mere thought of being exposed in front of an audience can lead to a reaction of closure and rejection of the training. In this case, virtual reality can be of great help. In addition to its great potential about the possibility of living a highly engaging and interactive experience, it allows precisely to expose the individual to the source of stress in a controlled environment: yes, because one is confronted in front of a virtual audience, simulated, but at the same time very close to reality. Another advantage is the possibility of creating different situations and simulations to enhance the person's ability to adapt; virtual reality also allows an assessment of the degree of use of the paralinguistic system, the so-called silent language (clothing, body gestures, and facial expressions). Several studies have considered the effectiveness of virtual reality in fear of public speaking. For example, research protocols were carried out to study the prototypical behavior of a real audience to design a virtual training scenario for fear of public speaking in a so-called CAVE, a cube-shaped immersive virtual room. This technology is considered the future in applications of this kind and more, but it must be remembered that it needs to be managed optimally to exploit its potential fully.

Another recent example is an application called "Ovation," made available for Oculus Rift and Vive, which offers a public speaking simulator and a result of tools. This technology allows the user to live a highly customizable experience, with the possibility of choosing the location, the type of audience, and the tools to be used (laser pointers, chalk, microphones, and blackboards). The critical aspect of Ovation is providing post-simulation analysis and objective indicators that offer instant feedback (quality of audience gaze and speaker hesitation). This is one of the fundamental advantages of using virtual reality, which, in addition to allowing training in protected and realistic contexts, gives the possibility of receiving instant analysis and feedback.

Using a sports metaphor, I would like to highlight the words of a great sportsman Kobe Bryant: "If you don't believe in yourself, who will?" This means that it is important to be a fan of yourself first. Otherwise, it will be difficult for others to be. If you believe in yourself, you will inspire other people, and they will believe in you much more quickly. Always remember, as I said at the beginning, that these skills have to be trained daily with commitment, perseverance, and the right motivation so that you can optimize them.

11.2 Stress in a World 3.0

As explained on other occasions, training refers to a learning process, an opportunity to change and improve oneself. One way could be to optimize one's ability to handle life's difficulties. Very often, these cause what in psychophysiology is called *stress*, which is the typical response of the individual to pressure from the environment (external and internal, physical, and psychic). Closely related to this, there is a way of acting that can be learned and optimized through training identified with the term *resilience*: the ability of the individual to cope with traumatic events and reorganize their life positively. Let us take a closer look at where these concepts and methods came from to optimize the management of the obstacles that life throws at us.

The first person to describe the bodily manifestations of stress was Darwin in 1872, referring to states of emotional and behavioral activation such as sweating, pupillary dilation, and tachycardia. Later, the most critical stress scholars were Cannon and Selye. The former, through studies on the digestive system of animals, created hypotheses on the body's reactions to situations of fear, danger, or pain. He introduced the concept of "fight or flight response" to describe the individual's behavior when faced with fear or threat as a fight or flight reaction. But the first to coin the word "stress" was Selye, who identified the response of the organism of animals and people to various stressors as the "general adaptation syndrome":

- *Alarm phase*: the immediate reaction of the organism that triggers a series of neurovegetative activations with the release of adrenaline and noradrenaline, activating the autonomic nervous system and, consequently, physiological changes aimed at self-preservation (attack or escape).
- *Resistance phase*: in this phase, the organism proceeds to a progressive adaptation and balance recovery.
- *Exhaustion phase*: this phase occurs when exposure to the stressor is prolonged. In this case, the organism enters a phase of exhaustion, the physiological changes giving rise to pathological consequences.

It is essential to point out that the body's response depends on how these stressors are perceived (real danger) or on expectations of threat that create anxiety (perception of risk). A distinction should be made here: stress is not always negative; on the contrary, we speak of eustress and distress. In the first case, it is an adaptive response to environmental conditions or events, which can save the individual's life in the face of real danger; in the second case, there is a condition of (real or perceived) imbalance between the stressor and the ability to cope with it. In the latter situation, the threat is generally of such a magnitude as to cause an emotional shock. It may lead to significant problems such as post-traumatic stress disorder and other stress-related distressing situations for the individual (stress disorders).

An attitude closely linked to this type of difficult situation, which allows the individual to regain his balance, is the resilient attitude. The studies on resilience arose from the observation of several children who, despite being exposed to various risk factors and consequently the high probability of subsequent psychosocial problems, still managed to form stable relationships in adulthood, committed to the world of work and their fellow human beings, thus leading a fulfilling life despite their torturous past. Scholars at this point wondered how it was possible to open up a strand of studies on the knowledge of prevention and protection factors that can influence proper development. The term resilience is used in physics to refer to a body that resists impact and returns to its original shape. In biology, it refers to the ability to repair oneself after damage. In psychology, resilience refers to "the ability of an individual to withstand the shocks of life without breaking or cracking while maintaining and enhancing his or her personal and social resources" (Oliverio Ferraris, 2003). It is also defined as "the ability to cope with stressful events, overcome them, and continue to develop by increasing one's resources with a consequent positive reorganization of life" (Malaguti, 2005). Thus, it could be said that resilience puts the individual in a position to grow and develop their potential effectively, even in the presence of risk factors and the above mentioned stressors. Beware of believing that resilience is an infallible and ubiquitous "weapon" because even resilient people can have difficulty overcoming trauma and other risk factors in life. Stress and resilience are two closely related concepts.

11.2.1 Managing Stress

What can be done to work on all of the above? Training can be created to support the individual to manage stress more effectively, perhaps at the same time working on learning to be resilient. Let us look at some examples together. The first thing I would like to draw your attention to is how to create interventions that promote resilience and stress management: it means it is good not to focus only on the specific problem but to always consider the needs, the resources of the person or group you are going to act on, and the context in which you are operating. In fact, for this very reason, the most effective approaches place the individual at the center of the process, starting precisely with their resources to strengthen them and acquire new ones. Experience is the driving force behind training in this area, as people can get involved and experience their emotions in contact with others through specific activities. The next step is to compare what happened and the resources used. A reflection contributing to becoming aware of what happens and what one can do to increase self-confidence is closely linked to resilience. Another method of promoting strength, although there are few studies in the literature, is storytelling. Writing about one's traumas is helpful for the person:

> The act of constructing a personal story helps people understand their experiences and themselves, as well as enables them to organize and remember events coherently by integrating thoughts and feelings. It gives people a sense of control over their lives because once they have structured and given meaning to their story, the emotional effects of the narrated experience become more manageable.

> **(Pennebaker & Seagal, 1999)**

Mental training techniques, such as relaxation, visualization, self-talk, and positive thinking, can significantly help in this field. Before explaining these techniques, I would like to explain what learning through mental training means.

11.2.2 *Let Us Train Ourselves in Sports-Mind*

Let us start with the definition of mental training: "the application of psychological techniques aimed at improving sporting performance as part of a structured program" (Cei, 1998). Mental training can be defined as psychological training consisting of a set of techniques and strategies that aim to acquire and enhance the athlete's mental calm and physical skills, which, together with the usual training program, help to improve the quality of sports performance of the user. At this point, you may ask, why do we talk about mental training for stress management? This customized training can also be built and applied in the workplace and everyday life, especially in today's society, where innovation is rampant and pressures are increasing; we often talk about performance, and higher and higher performance levels are required. Moreover, if we think of the emergency period we live in, things have changed, and so has our way of life.

The basis of mental training refers to two fundamental psychological concepts: cognitive modifiability and brain plasticity. The mediated learning experience refers to how a mediator selects, transforms, and shapes the stimuli experienced by the child, young person, adult, or older adult in the learning environment. Suppose the Mediated Learning Experience favors cognitive modifiability. In that case, the modifying climate is the context in which this modifiability becomes stable and can crystallize: this happens if the domain can stimulate it, a simultaneously welcoming and challenging setting capable of constantly creating new goals and objectives. Brain plasticity is closely related to modifiability: the ability of our nervous system to change due to environmental stimuli. "The brain can modify its *structure in response to experience*" (Siegel, 2012). However, the awareness of the possibility of modifying and creating new connections in the nervous system has yet to be recent. From a historical point of view, the concept of neuronal plasticity can be traced back to the end of the 19th century, underlining how learning, to be such, requires the formation of new connections between neurons (Cowan & Kandel, 2001; Berlucchi & Butchel, 2009). Mental training involves using specific techniques to strengthen cognitive abilities, including stress management. Let us see the main ones that lead the individual to optimize the response to the stimulus source of stress efficiently:

■ *Positive thinking*: the professional guides the person to identify what is positive in him and bring it out. The individual trains and accustoms the mind to produce helpful thoughts, change attitude, find a more effective, positive alternative point of view, and see "the glass half full." It is a conscious and functional re-orientation of thought as continuous training: moving the negative, seeing the positive, and blocking dark thoughts. Gradually, what seems to be an effort becomes natural; in this way, the user discovers that he has learned to think positively. Generally speaking, positive thinking is a philosophy of life, even before being a mental preparation technique. This critical mental training technique is complex and bizarre without such an inner approach or looking for the positive in others. This attitude fosters awareness of one's abilities and helps one use the appropriate means to overcome their limits. A direct consequence is the facilitation of optimal performance thanks to an effective self-management of emotions, in this case of n, negative and non-productive thoughts, such as anxiety and inadequacy. Positive thinking also promotes the development of cognitive restructuring capacity.

■ *Self-talk*: internal dialogue, vocalized or silent, made up of words, images, or positive thoughts to influence behavior. The person is trained to use "psychological reminders" of pictures or keywords to recall certain highly positive psychological feelings and states experienced in favorable circumstances. This technique can be aimed at developing new skills by focusing on essential aspects of performance linked to everyday life or the professional/sporting environment.

■ *Imagery or visualization*: the imaginative representation of specific situations related to the positive sphere in a setting full of positive stimuli. Successful mental evocation and projection help lower anxiety and stress levels, improve and correct certain mental automatisms (responses to stress), and consequently optimize the behavior in question.

■ *Relaxation*: relaxation controls the activation level to manage anxiety and psychophysical tension states. Relaxation techniques help achieve a psychophysical state of well-being and tranquility. Correct practice of these techniques allows the person to reach and maintain a better awareness and knowledge of himself, his body, and his emotions, through which he can modulate his state according to the demands of the performance and the situation. These procedures have a positive influence on anxiety and stress management.

Any training course in psychology also depends on the person's disposition towards these programs, which derives the level of commitment and constancy "in daily training."

11.2.3 Innovative Change

This stress training has changed, and more and more online training has to be designed. The most significant difficulty, in this case, is not being able to guarantee the active participation of the person: technology, in particular virtual reality, has come to our aid. Visors and advanced software allow us to create paths to strengthen individual resources (self-esteem, management of emotions) and rehabilitation paths, guaranteeing a high degree of interactivity and active experimentation.

For instance, virtual reality has been used to treat post-traumatic stress disorder, especially in the military. The guiding principle of this treatment seems to be the gradual re-introduction of the experiences that triggered the trauma. In practice, the patient is induced to re-live the traumatic situation gradually, but in a controlled context, without forcing the subject to face what he is not yet ready for. In this regard, the Institute for Creative Technologies (ICT) launched a project to create a system of virtual environments in which Iraq war veterans diagnosed with PTSD could be gradually immersed (Rizzo et al., 2006). More recently, this technology has also taken hold in cognitive rehabilitation (Gaggioli et al., 2009; Morganti & Riva, 2006). "Virtual rehabilitation" strongly increases the enjoyment, involvement, and motivation of the patient (Morganti, 2004), possessing the characteristics of intensity and repetitiveness typical of traditional protocols, with the part of being "task-oriented." A very recent example is the Cerebrum app, which allows the user to be immersed in experiential situations that simulate everyday reality, which is helpful to work on resources and difficulties of the users. Through the visor, users can view 360° videos, explore the scene, and answer the rehabilitation clinician's questions while allowing constant monitoring by the professional. Other applications in the literature show that training with mindfulness techniques mediated by wearable devices is practical in terms of neurocognitive enhancement and affective and stress regulation. A recent study shows that this affects car driving, reducing accidents considerably positively. The integration of the mindfulness technique, which included the use of neurofeedback and devices using Go/No-Go tasks in immersive virtual reality or the Active Box device for detecting driving behavior led to an increase in neural and behavioral efficiency in terms of speed of attention orientation, information processing, executive control, and a reduction in perceived fatigue and stress while driving.

So, what are the real advantages of virtual reality in this field? First, RV allows you to "practice" safely; just the thought of a stressful event is exhausting and debilitating, let alone reliving it for real. Thanks to virtual reality, the individual can face his difficulties in a controlled environment where he feels present and aware and can test his skills under the guidance of a professional. Moreover, virtual reality allows us to create specific situations to work with each one differently and personally. In addition, virtual reality allows practicing a particular task and simulating the activity repeatedly to enhance learning (Stinson & Bowman, 2014). It allows for the accurate and continuous collection of different data: eye movement can be tracked by eye trackers, and emotions can be followed by sensors measuring heartbeats, sweating, oxygenation, and facial expressions. All these advantages are generalizable to other areas of psychology. They can be summarized by the following concepts: transferability of learning, controlled environment, objective behavior measurement, visualization, and personalized treatment. The key aspect is that all factors involved in the interaction with new technologies can be controlled and manipulated, ensuring the reproducibility of the evidence.

I would like to conclude this chapter by stating that virtual reality is an essential means of prevention and learning, which allows one to live an experience directly, to "immerse" oneself in the concrete situation, virtually simulated. The content of this multisensory interface (involving sight, hearing, but also movement) allows participants to live individualized and emotionally involving experiences in a controlled context, learning from them and bringing them back to the natural environment (transferability of learning).

11.3 Emotional Intelligence

This paragraph will address a significant educational issue: emotional intelligence. Emotional intelligence is a fundamental part of intelligence, contributing to the pursuit of happiness and people's ability to adapt to their environment. Emotional intelligence refers to the ability to control and express one's emotions and understand, interpret, and respond to those of others. This is a very delicate concept, especially in a period like the one we live in today, where we have been forced to live in relationships at a distance to communicate in front of a screen without even being able to embrace each other. In addition, as we have already seen, it is always a complex matter when we talk about emotions since everyone can interpret them differently and needs help expressing specific experiences. But just think of a world where we cannot tell if a friend is happy, sad, or angry. Have you ever felt so overwhelmed by an emotion that you did something you later regretted? Emotional intelligence can help in these situations as a preventive tool and to cope with these moments. Let us examine how this concept came about and what can be done to optimize these skills.

The term emotional intelligence dates back to the 1930s when Edward Thorndike began talking about "social intelligence" as the ability of people to socialize and build stable bonds with people or within a group. Until the 1960s, however, the idea of intelligence had always been that of a unitary competence, capable of ensuring that humans could adapt to their environment and pursue goals. In the 1970s, with psychologist Howard Gardner, a new concept of intelligence emerged: no longer a single general factor but several "intelligence in the plural" (musical, linguistic, bodily, spatial, and mathematical). In the following years, the term "emotional intelligence" came into being, with an initial definition: "The ability to monitor one's own and other's emotions, to differentiate between them, and to use this information to guide one's thinking and actions" (Salovey & Mayer, 1990). Only five years later, Daniel Goleman concluded that it is still shared today: It is the ability to recognize our feelings and those of others, to motivate ourselves, and to manage our emotions positively, both internally and in social relationships. Two competencies would be identified, each with specific characteristics: on the one hand, personal competencies, including the ability to recognize and manage one's own emotions (self-awareness–self-mastery) and motivation to pursue goals, and on the other hand, social competencies, such as the ability to understand the feelings of others (empathy) and to create strong, positive bonds (social skills). In other words, emotional intelligence refers to different skills, such as empathy, motivation, self-control, logic, and the ability to adapt and manage one's own emotions and to find and succeed in using the positive aspects of every situation one encounters, which can be increasingly trained and optimized thanks to specific training courses. The skills that make up emotional intelligence are:

- emotional awareness, which is the ability to recognize and name one's own emotions in certain situations;
- dynamic control, that is, the control of emotions and impulses both toward oneself and toward others;
- the ability to know how to motivate oneself, that is, the ability to understand how to use emotions to achieve a goal;
- recognizing the feelings of others (empathy), that is, the ability to recognize the moods of others;
- effective management of interpersonal relationships is the ability to negotiate conflicts and communicate effectively.

Each component of emotional intelligence presented is related to our psychological well-being and can therefore be considered potential and improvable resources for our mental health. Let us show; let us see standard methods to improve these skills.

11.3.1 Traditional Mind Form vs. New Methods

According to Goleman, the pillar of emotional intelligence is according because it would be tough to intervene in aging and others' emotions without it. A traditional method for developing this capacity is the "emotional diary." This tool, which can also be used independently, allows you to answer a few simple questions to reconstruct the entire emotional event (what emotion, triggering event, reactions, and actions taken). The diary, if filled in once a day for at least a month, gives the person the opportunity to become more and more aware of their emotions and reactions while at the same time optimizing methods of managing them. Therefore, the first step to understanding what is happening inside ourselves and others is to write down this daily diary, which can be followed by a weekly delicate balance that shows us the course of our emotional reactions during the week. This is the basis for learning how to manage our emotions: one method to improve this skill is relaxation techniques, which can help to balance stress levels and impulses/reactions toward oneself or others. Relaxation techniques aim to achieve a specific psychophysical state, characterized by the perception of well-being, calm, and pleasure on the psychological side and muscle relaxation on the bodily side. Peace aims to control the activation level to manage anxiety and psychophysical tension states. Nervousness and anxiety are common emotions that everyone feels before an important event (exam, competition, meeting).

Moreover, different types of people place themselves along a continuum from low to high emotionality, particularly when they achieve success or worse when they fail. Whenever this happens, the person spends a lot of energy on their emotions and loses focus on their goal. Relaxation techniques, if appropriately trained and maintained continuously, have benefits for people:

- Reinforcement of self-esteem.
- Greater self-knowledge and better management of one's psychophysiological arousal (managing daily stress and emotional states such as performance anxiety and nervousness).
- Greater concentration on psychophysical changes during the day, modulating them to one's advantage.

The most commonly used relaxation techniques are Schultz's Autogenic Training (AT), Jacobson's Progressive Muscle Relaxation, and Biofeedback.

TA is a relaxation technique developed in the early 1900s by the German psychiatrist Johannes H. Schultz. Starting from hypnotic techniques and, in particular, from Oskar Vogt's research on sleep, Schultz developed a process that, unlike previous methods, aims to give the subject–patient a much more active and independent role from the therapist in achieving the state of relaxation. The technique consists of concentration exercises focusing on different body areas to gain a general physical and mental relaxation state. The characteristic aspect of this method is the possibility of obtaining, through activities to be considered "mental," natural changes in the body, which in turn affect the psychic sphere of the individual. All this is based on the basic assumption that a human organism is a biopsychic unit, according to which mind and body are not independent components but are interconnected in a relationship of mutual influence; therefore, a psychic modification causes changes in the organic level, and vice versa. The TA works according to the same logic of this approach: Schultz's concentration exercises are mainly studied and concatenated to progressively bring about actual organic modifications, precisely opposite to those produced by stress. All this leads to bodily relaxation, which consequently causes psychic relaxation. The six exercises that make up the technique are divided into lower and higher. In the former, mental attention is paid to particular bodily sensations, while in the latter, attention is paid to specific mental representations. The training of the higher exercises, because they address the mind and the unconscious, requires the presence of a therapist, while the lower exercises can also be performed alone. The first two levels are called fundamental, and the other four are complementary:

1. exercise of heaviness, which acts on the relaxation of the muscles;
2. the practice of warmth, which works on the dilation of peripheral blood vessels;
3. heart exercise, which works on cardiac function;
4. breath exercise, which works on the respiratory system;
5. solar plexus exercise, which works on the organs of the abdomen;
6. forehead exercise, which works on the brain.

The fundamental exercises help achieve deep relaxation, actively intervening in the mechanisms usually triggered automatically. Complementary activities, on the other hand, target a specific organ.

Edmund Jacobson developed progressive muscle relaxation (RMP) at the beginning of the last century and demonstrated the connection between high muscle tension and disorders of the body and psyche. He discovered that shortening the muscle fibers always accompanies muscle tension. At the same time, relaxation leads to a lengthening of the muscle fibers, a lowering of the activation of the sympathetic nervous system, and can be used as a remedy for psychosomatic disorders. RMP belongs to the category of muscle-to-mind relaxation, through which a state of relaxation is sought from bodily sensations. This procedure is based on the theory that states that relaxation and tension (this is derived from anxiety) are two opposite states and, therefore, cannot coincide. The technique involves the systematic and increasingly intense contraction of specific muscle groups, held in isometric tension for a few seconds before release. The contractions progressively and analytically involve all the muscle groups: arms, legs, torso, neck, and head. The procedure is considerably shortened, with training considering only the main muscle sectors. Through voluntary contraction, greater awareness and sensitivity to tense states are achieved; after the tension, the subsequent relaxation phase is experienced with greater intensity due to the contrasting effect. This game of continuous tension/relaxation allows you to focus on muscular activity, thus helping to increase your concentration levels. Comparing progressive muscle relaxation with autogenic training, they have fundamental differences and points of contact. The former is an "active" method, based on the contraction of different muscle sections (5–10 seconds) and then relaxing them to feel a feeling of heaviness and complete relaxation; the latter, on the other hand, involves a predisposition called "passive psychic concentration," in which one must learn to abandon oneself more deeply gradually and at the same time observe everything that happens at a psychosomatic level without interfering with these processes (the term "autogenous" refers to generating oneself, by oneself, without the help of the will). Both share the characteristics of the context in which the techniques are implemented. The environment must be quiet, comfortable, in half-light, and away from sound and visual stimuli. The clothing does not need any particularity; the only requirement is not to wear constricting objects such as watches, glasses, or shoes. The position assumed can also be in three ways: supine with legs apart and toes pointing outward, in an armchair, or a coachman's work on a chair.

A widely used tool, always with a view to relaxation and proprioception (knowledge of one's body), is biofeedback, which can be integrated with various relaxation techniques. Biofeedback is a tool with which people can become aware of their emotional problems and learn to control them spontaneously, thus becoming an active part of the therapeutic process. As a rule, people are unaware of many bodily functions, such as muscle relaxation, heartbeat, blood pressure, or gastric secretion, which the body performs automatically and involuntarily. The principle on which biofeedback is based is to optimize the subject's perception of these bodily activities by transmitting information about his biological and visceral functions and then training him to control them voluntarily.

So, in conclusion, we can say that relaxation techniques are voluntary actions to regulate and manage states of anxiety and stress, relieve the individual from tension, and restore his psychophysiological balance.

For example, it is essential to set goals. To improve the ability to self-motivate, a widely used technique from the world of sport, but applicable in all areas of our lives, is Goal Setting: "Setting goals is the first step in transforming the invisible into the visible" (Anthony Robbins). From this sentence, it can be deduced how important it is to set priorities that influence behavior and performance. However, objectives must have five specific characteristics to be effective. First, they must be precise and clear to eliminate uncertainties and sources of dispersion. Second, they must be measurable so that both the athlete and the psychologist can assess the progress of the course and make adjustments if necessary. Third, the goals must be accessible and realistic; they must refer to the concrete, not the abstract world. The fourth characteristic is the challenge: a plan must be challenging to keep the athlete's motivation high. Finally, the objective must always be linked to a precise time frame (short, medium, and long term). It is essential that flexible goals are formed in positive and proactive terms and that the psychologist takes into account all types of plans differentiating them: outcome goals (linked to the result), performance goals (related to the performance), process goals (related to the action, the technical gesture).

All these methods presented are some of the most famous traditional models that contribute to strengthening the skills that make up the emotional quotient. However, it is worth remembering that the effectiveness of these paths depends not only on the professional's skills but also on the willingness and perseverance of people to invest time and "effort" in their personal growth.

The new frontiers of training in emotional intelligence refer to a tool that is becoming more and more widespread and is virtual reality, thanks to which it is possible to carry out the activity in controlled and dynamic environments, lowering the barriers of fear about one's feelings, reactions and the judgment of others. Let us move into the world of education. The application of virtual reality is based on *Cooperative Learning*: these are learning paths in small groups, where pupils face different challenging tasks requiring other skills and work together to achieve common goals in a positive environment.

A practical example is the CROSSLessons, which combine the immersiveness and interactivity of virtual reality with the logical rigor of Problem-based Learning. The acronym CROSS refers to the five phases of the innovative teaching method and the skills to be developed:

■ *Challenge*: in this first phase, a challenge is posed to pupils through virtual reality (3D simulation of a scientific experiment, a virtual, historical, or geographical tour, or a VR film) that aims to stimulate curiosity and the ability to question problems and tackle them positively and fairly;
■ *Research*: this second phase refers to the competence to research and select information from different sources (books, web, personal ideas, etc.);
■ *Operate*: at this point, pupils can unleash their creativity, initiative, and inventiveness to create a virtual artifact;
■ *Say*: this is the exposure phase, where participants have the opportunity to train their communication skills in persuading others and convincing them of their ideas;
■ *Share*: in the final part of sharing and evaluating the products, participants learn to be willing to share their solutions with others, to question them, to review them, to consider, and to be reassessed. From the very name of the training course methodology, cooperative learning puts the individual in a position to develop, train, and optimize emotional intelligence in the network of relationships and social compromise for achieving specific goals.

As far as emotional education is concerned, *digital humanities*, that is, humanistic computing that approaches educational topics from an alternative, more modern, and closer to the world of digital native students, are increasingly used. One example is the use of tools such as ICT, that is, the use of digital technologies that lend themselves as a support to the classic didactic lesson to motivate learning and develop the student's social skills.

References

Airenti, G., Bara, B.G., & Colombetti, M. (1993). Failures, exploitations and deceits in communication. *Journal of Pragmatics*.

Anolli, L. (2002). *Psicologia della comunicazione*. Bologna: Il Mulino.

Anolli, L. et al. (2003). Linguistic styles in deceptive communication: Dubitative ambiguity and elliptic eluding in packaged lies. *Social Behavior and Personality*, 31(7), 687–710.

Anolli, L., Ciceri, R., & Riva, G. (2001). 4 seductive communication: Paradoxical exhibition, obliquity and non verbal synchronization. *Journal of Nonverbal Behavior*, 14, 209–236.

Anolli, L., Ciceri, R., & Riva, G. (2002). *Say not to say: New perspectives on miscommunication*. Amsterdam: IOS Press. Online: www.emergingcommunication .com/volume3.html.

Anolli, L., & Mantovani, F. (2011). *Come funziona la nostra mente. Apprendimento, simulazione e Serious Games*. Bologna: Il Mulino.

Berlucchi, G., & Butchel, H.A. (2009). Neuralplasticity: Historical roots and evolution of meaning. *Experimental Brain Research*, 192, 307–319.

Cei, A. (1998). *Psicologia dello sport*. Bologna: Il Mulino.

Chomsky, N. (1986). *Knowledge of language: Its nature, origin, and use*. New York: Praeger, Greenwood Publishing Group.

Cole, M. (1996). *Cultural psychology: A once and future discipline*. Cambridge, MA: Harvard University Press; trad. It. *La psicologia culturale: disciplina del passato e futura*. Rome: Edizioni Carlo Amore, 2006.

Cole, M., & Engeström, Y. (1993). A cultural-historical approach to distributed cognition. In G. Salomon (Ed.), *Distributed cognitions* (pp. 1–46). Cambridge: Cambridge University Press.

Cowan, W.M., & Kandel, E.R. (2001). A brief history of synapses and synaptic transmission. In W.M. Cowan, T.C. Sudhof, & C.F. Stevens, *Synapses* (pp. 1–87). Baltimore: The John Hopkins University Press.

Gaggioli, A. et al. (2009). *Advanced technologies in rehabilitation: Empowering cognitive, physical, social and communicative skills through virtual reality, robots, wearable systems and brain-computer interfaces*. Amsterdam: IOS Press.

Gibson, J. J. (1979). *The ecological approach to visual perception: Classic edition*. Hillsdale, NJ: Erlbaum; trad. It. *Un approccio ecologico alla percezione visiva*. Bologna: Il Mulino, 1999.

Kahneman, D. (2002). Maps of bounded rationality: A perspective on intuitive judgement and choice. In T. Frängsmyr (Ed.), *The Nobel Prizes 2002* (pp. 449–489). Stockholm: Nobel Foundation.

Lenggenhager, B. et al. (2007). Video ergo sum: Manipulating bodily self-consciousness.*Science*, 317(5841), 1096–1099.

Malaguti, E. (2005). *Educarsi alla resilienza: Come affrontare crisi e difficoltà e migliorarsi*. Gardolo di Trento: Edizioni Erickson.

Mantovani, G. (1996). *New communications environments: From everyday to virtual*. London: Taylor & Francis.

Morganti, F., & Riva, G. (2006). *Conoscenza, comunicazione e tecnologia: Aspetti cognitivi della realtà virtuale*. Milan: LED Edizioni Universitarie.

Morganti, F. (2004). Virtual interaction in cognitive neuropsychology. In G. Riva & Bottega et al. (Eds.) (pp. 85–101). Online: www.cybertherapy.info/pages/book3.htm.

Oliverio Ferraris, A. (2003). *La forza d'animo.* Milan: Rizzoli.

Pacherie, E. (2006). Toward a dynamic theory of intentions. In S. Pocket, W.P. Banks, & S. Gallagher (Eds.), *Does consciousness cause behavior?* (pp. 145–167). Cambridge, MA: MIT Press.

Pennebaker, J.W., & Seagal, J.D. (1999). Forming a story: The health benefits of narrative. *Journal of Clinical Psychology,* 55(10), 1243–1254.

Riva, G. (2007). Virtual reality and telepresence. *Science,* 318(5854), 1240–1242.

Riva, G. (2010). *I social network.* Bologna: Il Mulino.

Riva, G. (2012). *Psicologia dei nuovi media. Azione, presenza, identità e relazioni.* Bologna: Il Mulino.

Riva, G., & Davide, F. (2001). *Communications through virtual technologies: Identity, community and technology in the communication age.* Amsterdam: IOS Press. Online: www.emergingcommunication.com/volume5.html.

Salovey, P., & Mayer, J.D. (1990). Emotional intelligence. *Imagination, Cognition and Personality,* 9(3), 185–211.

Shannon, C.E., & Weaver, W. (1949). *The mathematical theory of communication.* Urbana: University of Illinois Press.

Siegel, D.J. (2012). *La mente relazionale Neurobiologia dell'esperienza interpersonale.* Milano: Raffaello Cortina Editore.

Skinner, B.F. (1957). *Verbal behavior.* New York: Appleton-Century-Crofts.

Tessarolo, T. (2007). *Net Tv. Come Internet cambierà la televisione per sempre.* Milano: Apogeo Editore.

Watzlawick, P. (1976). *La realtà della realtà: Comunicazione disinformazione confusione.* Rome: Astrolabio.

LEVERAGING YOUR BUSINESS

Chapter 12

Immersive Experiences and Intelligent Insights

Soft skills are crucial for personal and professional success, but developing them can be challenging. However, combining VR and AI technologies offers exciting opportunities to cultivate and enhance soft skills. This chapter explores how VR and AI can be leveraged to develop essential soft skills, providing immersive experiences and intelligent insights to foster growth and mastery (Figure 12.1). The technology is running fast, with the presence on the market of ChatGPT and the access to their API, and the integration of generative AI projects that now are available on the web, they can be integrated into the VR. The combination of both technologies, VR and AI, will leverage an immersive experience that we have never seen before.

12.1 Communication and Collaboration

VR simulations offer a realistic setting for honing communication and teamwork abilities. Participants in coaching sessions can interact in computer-generated simulations of real-world situations like team meetings, negotiations, or consumer encounters. Their ability to communicate effectively through verbal and non-verbal cues, active listening, and empathy can be assessed by AI-powered analysis. Coachees get immediate feedback, which helps them improve their abilities and boost confidence in their

DOI: 10.4324/9781003439691-16

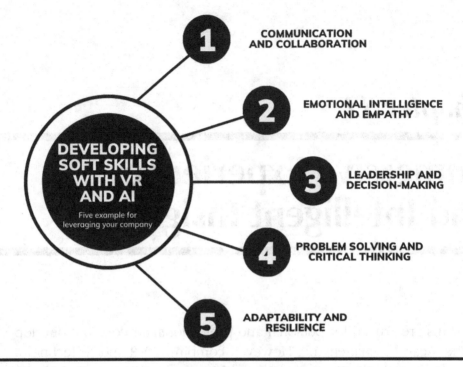

Figure 12.1 Five points for leveraging your business. Personal elaboration.

capacity for collaboration and communication, for instance, the integration of software that can recognize the tone of the voice and give feedback based on the situation and experience.

12.1.1 Immersive Communication Scenarios

VR simulations can mimic actual communication situations, enabling coachees to hone their communication abilities in a secure setting. Coachees may participate in virtual team meetings, client presentations, or public speaking competitions. They can better communicate their thoughts clearly and succinctly and modify their communication style for various audiences. Through VR, coachees can better understand the mechanics of interpersonal communication, including non-verbal cues, body language, and eye contact. Moreover, it is important to create environments where individuals feel secure enough to take risks and learn from their mistakes and pursue growth without the pressure of external criticism. The absence of fear of judgment encourages open communication, creativity, and resilience, leading to more productive and open working environments.

12.1.2 Feedback and Analysis

AI algorithms can analyze coachees' communication patterns and provide detailed feedback based on the data collected from VR simulations. By tracking speech patterns, tone, and part of body language, AI can assess the clarity of their messages, their ability to actively listen, and their level of empathy and understanding. This intelligent analysis helps coachees identify areas for improvement and provides specific recommendations to enhance their communication skills.

12.1.3 Cross-Cultural Communication

VR and AI technologies also offer opportunities for practicing cross-cultural communication. VR simulations can recreate diverse cultural scenarios, enabling coachees to experience and navigate cultural differences in communication styles, norms, and expectations. AI algorithms can provide insights and guidance on adapting communication approaches to different cultural contexts, promoting intercultural understanding and effective communication across diverse environments.

12.1.4 Team Collaboration and Conflict Resolution

VR environments can simulate team collaboration and conflict resolution scenarios, allowing coachees to practice effective teamwork and conflict management skills. Coachees can engage in virtual team projects, requiring them to collaborate, delegate tasks, and resolve conflicts that may arise. AI algorithms can assess their ability to foster teamwork, facilitate effective collaboration, and mediate disputes. This feedback-driven approach empowers coachees to develop essential collaboration skills and enhances their ability to work effectively in team settings.

Integrating VR and AI technologies in communication and collaboration training offers transformative possibilities for skill development. By providing immersive experiences, intelligent feedback, and personalized analysis, VR and AI empower coachees to enhance communication effectiveness, adapt to diverse cultural contexts, collaborate effectively in teams, and cultivate empathy and active listening skills. Through continuous practice and targeted feedback, individuals can develop strong communication and collaboration capabilities that positively impact their personal and professional interactions.

BOX 12.1: CASE STUDY—A CLEAR COMMUNICATION AND BIAS AS BARRIER

Clear communication involves techniques that will get you heard and understood and enable you to influence others: distinguish between good and bad communication practices and apply precise communication techniques and behavior in a practical scenario. Let's analyze a case study published by Bodyswaps.

The scenario is simple: You have been working with Daniel on a project that Sonya oversees. The delivery is due tomorrow, but something came up, and you need an extension. Daniel could do a better job of communicating what happened and what you need. Your first task is to observe Daniel and identify poor communication practices. Then, you can explain the situation face-to-face with Sonya and request a delay.

The second simulation realized by Bodyswaps is Bias as Barrier. Through this scenario, you will witness how your thinking is shaped by unconscious bias; explore your own experiences of discrimination; critically examine bias in popular media; and identify and challenge your preference.

Biases are a natural part of how our brains operate. They are essential. Only when we allow them to impact others negatively do they become a problem.

This simulation explores where biases come from and how they affect us and demonstrates valuable strategies and techniques for identifying challenging times when we might be thinking or acting from a biased point of view (Bodyswaps, 2022).

12.2 Emotional Intelligence and Empathy

Developing emotional intelligence and empathy can only be challenging with real-life experiences. VR can create immersive scenarios that simulate emotional situations, enabling coachees to navigate and respond appropriately to different emotional cues. This combination of VR and AI facilitates the development of emotional intelligence by offering opportunities to practice and refine empathetic responses in a controlled environment.

12.2.1 *Immersive Emotional Scenarios*

VR simulations can create immersive scenarios that elicit various emotions, allowing coachees to practice recognizing and managing emotions in a controlled environment. For instance, coachees can engage in virtual methods that involve challenging conversations, conflict resolution, or emotionally charged situations. Through these simulations, coachees can develop self-awareness, recognize their emotional responses, and learn to regulate and express emotions effectively.

12.2.2 *Perspective-Taking and Empathy Training*

VR can facilitate perspective-taking and empathy training by placing coachees in the shoes of others. By embodying different virtual characters and experiencing their perspectives, coachees can develop a deeper understanding of diverse experiences and cultivate empathy. AI can analyze the coachees' responses and provide feedback on their empathetic knowledge and expression. This feedback-driven approach enables coachees to refine their empathetic skills and foster more meaningful connections with others.

12.2.3 *Non-Verbal Communication and Emotional Expression*

Non-verbal communication plays a crucial role in emotional intelligence and empathy. VR simulations can offer opportunities for coachees to practice recognizing and interpreting non-verbal cues, such as facial expressions, body language, and tone of voice. Coachees can engage in virtual conversations where they must accurately interpret and respond to these cues. AI algorithms can analyze the coachees' performance and provide feedback on their ability to effectively understand and respond to non-verbal signals. There is still lots of work to do in terms of hardware development and graphic design, but the more the hardware and graphic design improves, the better the feedback and the simulations will respond.

12.2.4 *Emotional Regulation and Stress Management*

Emotional intelligence encompasses the ability to regulate one's emotions and manage stress. VR simulations can create stress-inducing scenarios, allowing coachees to practice emotional regulation techniques in a safe and controlled environment. Coachees can learn strategies such as deep breathing, cognitive reframing, and mindfulness to manage stress and maintain emotional balance. AI analysis can provide feedback on their effectiveness in regulating emotions and offer personalized recommendations for improvement.

12.2.5 *Cultural Competence and Empathetic Cross-Cultural Interactions*

VR and AI can also contribute to developing cultural competence and empathetic cross-cultural interactions. VR simulations can recreate diverse cultural scenarios, enabling coachees to navigate and understand cultural differences in emotions, expressions, and communication styles. AI algorithms can analyze the coachees' responses and provide insights on adapting empathetic approaches to different cultural contexts. This fosters intercultural understanding, reduces biases, and promotes effective cross-cultural communication.

Combining VR and AI technologies presents a unique opportunity to develop emotional intelligence and empathy. By immersing coachees in realistic dynamic scenarios, facilitating perspective-taking, analyzing non-verbal communication, practicing emotional regulation, and fostering cultural competence, VR and AI enable coachees to develop these vital skills dynamically and engagingly. Integrating immersive experiences and intelligent feedback creates a powerful platform for cultivating emotional intelligence and empathy, ultimately enhancing interpersonal relationships, communication effectiveness, and overall personal and professional growth.

12.3 Leadership and Decision-Making

VR and AI technologies can enhance leadership and decision-making skills by creating dynamic and challenging scenarios. Coachees can engage in virtual leadership simulations that require them to make critical decisions, manage teams, and resolve conflicts. AI algorithms can evaluate their decision-making processes, analyze leadership styles, and provide feedback on areas for improvement. Coachees can develop and refine their leadership abilities by repeatedly engaging in VR simulations and receiving personalized feedback.

12.3.1 *Virtual Leadership Simulations*

VR simulations can create virtual scenarios where coachees can practice and refine their leadership skills. These simulations can involve leading a team, making critical decisions, managing conflicts, or dealing with complex situations. Coachees can experience the challenges and dynamics of leadership in a controlled environment, allowing them to develop confidence and competence in their leadership abilities.

12.3.2 Dynamic and Challenging Decision-Making Scenarios

VR can present coachees with dynamic and challenging decision-making scenarios that require critical thinking and practical decision-making skills. These simulations can replicate real-life situations with multiple stakeholders, limited information, and time constraints. Coachees can practice evaluating alternatives, analyzing risks and benefits, and making sound decisions. AI algorithms can analyze their decision-making processes and provide feedback on their approach, helping them enhance their decision-making abilities.

12.3.3 Leadership Style Analysis

AI can analyze coachees' behavior and decision-making patterns in VR simulations to assess their leadership styles. By evaluating communication patterns, team interactions, and the coachees' responses to different challenges, AI can provide insights into their leadership strengths and areas for improvement. This analysis helps coachees understand and adapt their leadership style to different situations, fostering their growth as influential leaders.

12.3.4 Feedback and Continuous Improvement

AI-powered analysis can offer real-time feedback during VR simulations, guiding coachees toward more effective leadership and decision-making practices. Coachees can receive instant feedback on their communication approaches, problem-solving strategies, and leadership effectiveness. This enables them to adjust, experiment with different methods, and continuously improve their leadership skills in a supportive, learning-focused environment.

12.3.5 Team Collaboration and Conflict Management

VR simulations can also focus on team collaboration and conflict management, crucial aspects of leadership. Coachees can engage in virtual team projects or challenging team dynamics scenarios to navigate conflicts, motivate team members, and foster collaboration. AI algorithms can assess their ability to build and manage high-performing teams, mediate disputes, and delegate tasks effectively. The feedback provided by AI analysis supports coachees in developing strong leadership skills and creating cohesive and productive teams.

12.4 Problem-Solving and Critical Thinking

VR environments can be designed to present complex problems and challenges, providing coachees with opportunities to develop problem-solving and critical thinking skills. Through interactive simulations, coachees can practice analyzing situations, considering multiple perspectives and developing creative solutions. AI algorithms can evaluate their problem-solving approaches, identify strengths and weaknesses, and offer insights for improvement. This iterative process of problem-solving in VR, supported by AI analysis, promotes the development of robust critical thinking skills.

12.4.1 Complex Problem Scenarios

VR simulations can present coachees with complex and realistic problem scenarios, challenging them to think critically and find creative solutions. These simulations can replicate real-life situations that require analytical thinking, creativity, and practical problem-solving strategies. Coachees can engage in interactive problem-solving exercises, exploring different approaches, and evaluating their outcomes, for example, by creating different levels of complexity and, at each level, increasing the combination of difficulties.

12.4.2 Analytical Thinking and Data Analysis

AI can analyze the coachees' problem-solving approaches in VR simulations, assessing their analytical thinking skills and data analysis capabilities. AI provides valuable feedback on enhancing their analytical thinking skills by evaluating their ability to gather and interpret information, identify patterns, and draw logical conclusions. This analysis supports coachees in developing a systematic and evidence-based approach to problem-solving.

12.4.3 Divergent and Convergent Thinking

VR simulations can foster both divergent and convergent thinking, essential components of effective problem-solving and critical thinking. Coachees can brainstorm sessions within virtual environments, generating ideas and exploring different perspectives.

12.4.4 Cognitive Flexibility and Adaptability

VR and AI technologies can also promote cognitive flexibility and adaptability in problem-solving. VR simulations can introduce unexpected variables or changing circumstances, challenging coachees to adapt their thinking and problem-solving strategies. AI analysis can assess the coachees' ability to handle ambiguity, respond to unexpected challenges, and adjust their problem-solving approaches accordingly. This feedback-driven approach fosters adaptability and equips coachees with the skills to tackle complex and uncertain problems.

12.4.5 Reflection and Iterative Improvement

VR and AI facilitate reflection and iterative improvement in problem-solving and critical thinking. Coachees can review their performance in VR simulations and receive AI-generated feedback on their problem-solving strategies, identifying strengths and areas for improvement. This reflective process enables coachees to refine their thinking, experiment with different approaches, and continuously enhance their problem-solving and critical thinking abilities.

VR and AI technologies provide a powerful platform for developing problem-solving and critical thinking skills. Individuals can cultivate robust problem-solving and critical thinking abilities by engaging in immersive problem scenarios, analyzing data, fostering divergent and convergent thinking, promoting cognitive flexibility, and facilitating reflection and iterative improvement. These skills are essential for navigating complex challenges, making informed decisions, and driving innovation in various personal and professional domains. Integrating VR and AI offers a transformative approach to problem-solving and critical thinking development, preparing individuals to thrive in today's dynamic and ever-evolving world.

12.5 Adaptability and Resilience

VR and AI technologies can be powerful tools for developing adaptability and resilience, skills essential in an ever-changing world. VR simulations can expose coachees to scenarios that require adaptability, such as handling unexpected challenges of managing ambiguity. AI algorithms can analyze their responses and provide feedback on adaptability and resilience strategies. Coachees can practice adapting to different circumstances and receive guidance on building resilience, equipping them with the skills to navigate complex and uncertain environments.

12.5.1 Dynamic and Challenging Environments

VR simulations can replicate dynamic and challenging environments that require adaptability and resilience. Coachees can engage in virtual scenarios that mimic real-world situations characterized by uncertainty, ambiguity, and unexpected changes. By navigating these simulated environments, coachees can develop the ability to quickly adapt their strategies, make agile decisions, and maintain composure under pressure.

12.5.2 Stress and Emotion Regulation

VR can create stress-inducing scenarios, allowing coachees to practice stress and emotion regulation techniques. These simulations can present coachees with high-pressure situations, triggering emotional responses and stress. By practicing strategies such as deep breathing, mindfulness, and cognitive reframing within VR, coachees can learn to regulate their emotions and manage stress effectively. AI analysis can provide feedback on their stress management techniques, helping them refine their coping strategies.

12.5.3 Cognitive Flexibility

VR and AI technologies can enhance cognitive flexibility, enabling coachees to adapt their thinking and approaches in different contexts. VR simulations can introduce unexpected variables or changing circumstances, requiring coachees to think creatively, adjust their strategies, and consider alternative solutions. AI analysis can assess their cognitive flexibility, providing feedback on their ability to think adaptively and consider multiple perspectives.

12.5.4 Resilience Building

VR simulations can provide opportunities for coachees to develop resilience by presenting them with challenging situations and setbacks. Coachees can engage in virtual scenarios that require perseverance, problem-solving, and bouncing back from failures. AI can analyze their responses and provide feedback on building resilience, encouraging them to learn from setbacks, embrace a growth mindset, and persist in adversity.

12.5.5 Feedback and Reflection

AI analysis in VR simulations can offer valuable feedback on adaptability and resilience skills. Coachees can review their performance, receive personalized insights on their adaptive strategies, and identify areas for improvement. The feedback-driven approach allows coachees to reflect on their experiences, learn from their actions, and iterate their procedures to enhance their adaptability and resilience.

VR and AI technologies provide powerful tools for developing adaptability and resilience skills. By immersing coachees in dynamic environments, facilitating stress and emotion regulation, fostering cognitive flexibility, building resilience, and offering feedback and reflection, VR and AI empower individuals to navigate uncertainty and change with agility and strength. These skills are essential for personal growth, professional success, and well-being in an ever-evolving world. Integrating VR and AI in coaching offers a transformative approach to cultivating adaptability and resilience, equipping individuals with the tools to thrive in challenging circumstances and embrace change as an opportunity for growth.

To summarize this chapter, soft skills are vital for success in personal and professional contexts, and VR and AI offer innovative ways to develop and enhance these skills. Through immersive experiences and intelligent insights, VR simulations provide realistic practice environments, while AI analysis offers personalized feedback and guidance. By utilizing VR and AI technologies, individuals can cultivate essential soft skills such as communication, collaboration, emotional intelligence, leadership, problem-solving, adaptability, and resilience. Integrating VR and AI in soft skills development opens up exciting possibilities for accelerated growth, enabling individuals to thrive in a rapidly changing world. Of course, this is just the beginning, and creating simulations with VR and AI can be more accessible and more manageable with technological progress.

Reference

Bodyswaps. (2022). Bodyswaps®. Available at: https://bodyswaps.co/soft-skills-train-ing-in-vr/lets-talk-about-race/bias-as-a-barrier/.

Chapter 13

Data-Driven Coaching

Data has become a significant resource in the digital age that may generate insights and guide decision-making. Coaching is no exception since AI can use data to give coaches and coachees insightful information. The coaching process can be improved, and personal and professional progress can be supported by AI algorithms that examine patterns, trends, and behaviors. The idea of data-driven coaching is reviewed in this chapter, along with the various applications of AI that can yield insightful data. It is possible to evaluate the evidence that it is ready and tested in other projects in virtual reality (VR) as well (Figure 13.1).

13.1 The Power of Data in Coaching

Data plays a pivotal role in coaching, providing valuable insights, and driving informed decision-making. By leveraging AI algorithms to analyze patterns, trends, and behaviors, coaches can better understand their coachees and tailor their interventions more effectively.

Here are some key aspects highlighting the power of data in coaching.

13.1.1 Enhanced Understanding of Coachees

Coaches can develop a thorough grasp of their coachees through data-driven coaching. Coaches can learn about their coachees' talents, shortcomings, preferences, and aspirations using various data sources, including evaluations, questionnaires, performance measures, and self-reflection. This

 DOI: 10.4324/9781003439691-17

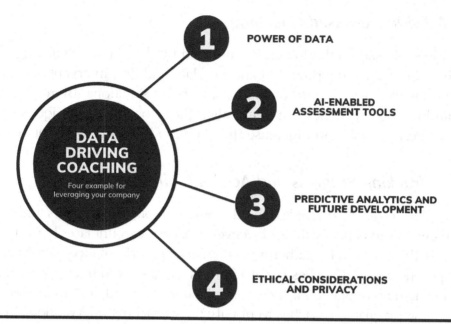

Figure 13.1   Four points for leveraging your business. Personal elaboration.

all-encompassing perspective aids coaches in identifying areas for development, investigating prospective growth prospects, and creating focused coaching interventions.

13.1.2 Objective Assessment and Feedback

Data-driven coaching enables coaches to provide objective assessments and feedback to coachees. AI algorithms can process and analyze collected data, removing biases and subjectivity. This objectivity helps coaches deliver feedback based on concrete evidence and provides a clearer understanding of performance, strengths, and areas requiring development. This data-driven feedback supports self-awareness and goals.

13.1.3 Informed Decision-Making

Coaches can decide on coaching tactics and interventions with confidence, thanks to data. They can spot patterns, trends, and correlations in data that might not be obvious at first glance. They can modify their coaching strategies to meet their coachees' requirements, preferences, and learning preferences. Coaches can design tailored coaching programs that are more likely to provide results (Marsh & Farrell, 2015).

13.1.4 Evidence-Based Coaching

An evidence-based methodology is embraced by data-driven coaching. Coaches can use AI algorithms to analyze data and find interventions and strategies with a track record of success in similar situations. By relying on data and research, coaches can better align their coaching techniques with industry best practices and increase the likelihood of successful outcomes.

13.1.5 Tracking Progress and Accountability

Data enables coaches to monitor the development of their students and hold them accountable for their objectives. Coaches can unbiasedly measure growth over time by gathering and analyzing performance metrics and other pertinent data. Coaches benefit from this data-driven tracking because it keeps them accountable for their commitments, focused, and motivated. Furthermore, it enables coaches to modify their coaching interventions in light of current insights, encouraging a flexible and responsive coaching process.

13.1.6 Continuous Improvement

A culture of continuous improvement is encouraged by data-driven coaching. Coaches can spot trends, assess the success of their coaching strategies, and make necessary corrections by routinely gathering and analyzing data. Coaches can improve their coaching methods, develop their skills, and provide even more effective coaching experiences by using this iterative process of data-driven reflection and improvement.

Data's importance for coaching must be balanced. Coaches can develop a deeper understanding of their coachees, offer unbiased assessments and feedback, make wise decisions, monitor progress, and promote accountability by utilizing AI algorithms to analyze data. Data-driven coaching improves the coaching process, encourages the use of proven techniques, and fosters ongoing development. Using data, coaches can create transformative coaching experiences that promote their coachees' personal and professional development.

13.2 AI-Enabled Assessment Tools

AI-enabled assessment tools are revolutionizing the coaching industry by giving coaches advanced tools for obtaining and analyzing data. The assessment process is improved, and coaches are given the information they need to make wise decisions. These tools use AI algorithms to extract insightful data from various assessment methods.

13.2.1 Intelligent Insights and Analysis

AI algorithms can analyze assessment data at a sophisticated level that surpasses manual analysis. These algorithms can find correlations, patterns, and trends that may be challenging for coaches to spot independently. AI-enabled assessment tools give coaches intelligent insights that support a deeper understanding of coachees' strengths, areas for improvement, and underlying behaviors by processing large volumes of data quickly and accurately.

13.2.2 Personalized Assessment

Assessment tools with AI capabilities can tailor the evaluation process to each coachee. These tools guarantee the assessment procedure is specialized and pertinent by adjusting to coachees' particular needs, preferences, and developmental objectives. This personalization improves the assessment's precision and efficacy and produces more insightful and valuable results.

13.2.3 Automated Data Collection and Analysis

Assessment tools with AI capabilities streamline the gathering and analysis of data. These tools automate the data entry and analysis processes, saving time and minimizing human error. Rather than becoming overwhelmed by the administrative aspects of assessment, coaches can concentrate more on interpreting the results and offering insightful commentary. Because of their increased effectiveness, coaches can assess their charges more frequently and consistently, making tracking their development more accessible (Majeed & Hwang, 2021).

13.2.4 Comprehensive and Holistic Assessment

AI-enabled assessment tools can give a thorough and all-encompassing overview of coachees' skills, preferences, and developmental requirements. These tools can integrate multiple assessment techniques, including self-assessments, 360° feedback, personality tests, and performance metrics.

Combining various data sources allows AI algorithms to understand better the coachees' strengths, weaknesses, and potential growth areas. This thorough assessment improves the accuracy and depth of coaching.

13.2.5 Real-Time Feedback and Reporting

Assessment tools with AI capabilities provide real-time feedback and reporting options. Coaches can provide timely and pertinent feedback to coachees because they can access immediate results and insights. Real-time feedback improves coaching by enabling coaches to quickly address specific issues, monitor progress, and modify coaching strategies. Additionally, AI-enabled assessment tools can produce automated reports that compile assessment results, simplifying the review and discussion of the results for coaches and coachees.

13.2.6 Continuous Learning and Improvement

Assessment tools that use AI have the potential to grow and learn over time. As more data is gathered and analyzed, AI algorithms can improve their analysis methods, unearth fresh insights, and adjust to shifting coaching requirements. By ensuring that assessment tools develop and become more precise and efficient over time, coaches are better able to provide high-quality assessments and interventions.

AI-enabled assessment tools are revolutionizing the coaching landscape by giving coaches intelligent insights, personalized assessment experiences, automated data collection and analysis, thorough assessments, real-time feedback, and continuous learning capabilities. With the aid of these tools, the assessment process is improved, allowing coaches to collect, analyze, and make decisions based on data more efficiently. By utilizing AI algorithms, they can better understand their coachees' abilities, preferences, and developmental needs, ultimately resulting in more focused and effective coaching interventions. The assessment phase of the coaching journey is made more accurate, efficient, and effective by AI-enabled assessment tools, which are priceless additions to the coaching toolkit.

13.3 Predictive Analytics and Future Development

Predictive analytics is a potent use of AI in coaching, which enables coaches to foresee potential development areas and take proactive measures.

Predictive analytics can offer helpful insights into coachees' possible growth trajectories and assist coaches in creating strategies to support their future development by examining historical data and patterns.

13.3.1 Forecasting Performance and Progress

Predictive analytics uses AI algorithms to analyze historical data and find trends that can be used to predict coachees' future performance and progress. Predictive analytics can inform coaches about their coachees' potential growth trajectory by looking at past accomplishments, behavioral patterns, and developmental milestones. Thanks to this forecasting capability, coaches can proactively identify areas where coachees may experience difficulties or need additional support.

13.3.2 Anticipating Developmental Needs

Coaches, with the aid of predictive analytics, anticipate coachees' needs. Coaches can gain insights into areas where coachees may need further development by examining patterns in historical data, such as past performance, assessment results, and learning progress. Due to their foresight, coaches can create personalized coaching plans that cater to the needs of individual coachees in terms of their developmental stages, ensuring that they get the targeted interventions they need to advance.

13.3.3 Tailoring Coaching Strategies

Coaches can customize their coaching strategies using predictive analytics based on anticipated development areas. Coaches can proactively modify their coaching approaches, methodologies, and interventions to suit coachees' changing needs by being aware of the potential growth trajectories of their charges. By focusing on the particular areas that are essential for coachees' future success, this specialized approach ensures that coaching remains applicable and practical.

13.3.4 Preventing Potential Challenges

Coaches can identify potential difficulties or obstacles that coachees might experience on their developmental journey with predictive analytics. By analyzing historical data and patterns, coaches can anticipate potential barriers and create interventions to avoid or lessen them. With this proactive approach, coaches can equip their students with the skills they will need to overcome obstacles and keep up their forward progress.

13.3.5 Iterative Improvement and Optimization

Using data-driven insights, predictive analytics enables coaches to improve and optimize their coaching interventions continuously. Coaches can spot areas where modifications to their coaching strategies can be made by analyzing the results of previous interventions and comparing them to expected outcomes. The coaching approaches evolve to the future developmental requirements of the coachees', thanks to this iterative improvement process.

13.3.6 Empowering Coachees

By giving coachees a better understanding of their potential growth trajectory, predictive analytics can empower them. Coaches can assist coachees in setting reasonable expectations and goals by providing information about their future development areas. Knowing that their coaches have a data-driven understanding of their potential can give coachees confidence and motivation, encouraging a sense of ownership and commitment to their personal and professional development.

13.4 Ethical Considerations and Privacy

As AI becomes increasingly integrated into coaching practices, it is crucial to address ethical considerations and prioritize privacy to ensure data's responsible and ethical use.

13.4.1 Data Privacy and Confidentiality

In AI-enabled coaching, maintaining data privacy and confidentiality is crucial. Coaches ensure that sensitive and private data is collected, transmitted, and stored securely. This entails putting strong data protection measures in place, abiding by pertinent data protection laws, and getting coachees' informed consent for data collection and usage. Additionally, coaches must be open and honest with coachees about how their data will be used, who will have access to it, and why.

13.4.2 *Informed Consent and Transparency*

Coaches must obtain coachees' informed consent before collecting or using their data. The types of data being gathered, how they will be analyzed, and how they will influence the coaching process should all be fully disclosed to the coachees. To ensure that coachees can make thoughtful decisions about participating in data-driven coaching interventions, clear communication about the capabilities and limitations of AI-enabled coaching tools is essential.

13.4.3 *Bias and Fairness*

The biases present in the data they are trained on may be reflected in the AI algorithms used in coaching. Coaches need to be conscious of these potential biases and take action to lessen their effects. Identifying and correcting any likely preferences includes routinely auditing and monitoring AI systems. Coaches should also ensure that coaching decisions and interventions are impartial and devoid of bias, both in designing AI algorithms and in their interpretation and use.

13.4.4 *Human Oversight and Interpretation*

Even though AI can offer insightful analysis and recommendations, humans must still oversee and interpret the coaching process. Coaches should use AI algorithms to support their expertise and judgment rather than relying solely on them. Human coaches crucially understand the context, nuances, and complexity of coaching relationships, and they should use professional judgment when interpreting data and offering coaching interventions.

13.4.5 *Responsible Use of Data*

The use of the data by coaches must be ethical and responsible. Without the coachees' consent, data should only be used for coaching and never be shared or used for unrelated purposes. Coaches should also be aware of the potential repercussions of sharing data with outside AI service providers and ensure that the necessary data protection agreements are in place to protect the information of their coachees.

13.4.6 Continuous Monitoring and Evaluation

Ethical issues and privacy should be constantly monitored and assessed in AI-enabled coaching practices. Coaches should stay current on industry best practices and changing data protection regulations. To ensure compliance and preserve the trust and integrity of the coaching relationship, it is essential to regularly assess the ethical implications of using AI in coaching and the impact on coachees' privacy.

In conclusion, AI-powered data-driven coaching presents unheard-of opportunities to use knowledge and improve the coaching process. AI can support the development of coachees by collecting and analyzing data, offering individualized feedback and recommendations, and enabling the objective measurement of progress. AI-enabled assessment tools, predictive analytics, and adaptive coaching interventions improve the coaching experience by providing deeper insights and foreseeing future development areas. However, it is crucial to prioritize data privacy and security and consider ethical issues. Ultimately, combining human coaches with AI technology can produce a potent synergy that enhances coaching results and enables people to reach their full potential.

References

Majeed, A., & Hwang, S.O. (2021). *Data-driven analytics leveraging artificial intelligence in the era Covid-19: An insightful review of recent developments.* MDPI. Available at: https://www.mdpi.com/2073-8994/14/1/16.

Marsh, J.A., & Farrell, C.C. (2015). *How leaders can support teachers with data-driven decision making: A framework for understanding capacity building.* Available at: http://hillkm.com/Unit_5_Marsh_2015.pdf.

Chapter 14

The Future of Coaching

Coaching is a vital component of personal and professional development. It aims to help individuals achieve their goals and reach their full potential. The coaching world is changing with the emergence of VR and AI. This chapter will explore how VR and AI are changing the coaching world and their impact on coaches and clients.

VR technology is increasingly used in coaching to create immersive learning experiences. Coaches leverage VR to create simulations that allow their clients to practice real-life scenarios and develop their skills in a safe and controlled environment. For example, athletes can use VR simulations to practice and improve their techniques, while business executives can use VR simulations to practice public speaking or negotiations. VR coaching sessions are also more engaging and interactive, making them more effective for clients.

AI is also transforming the coaching world by providing coaches with valuable insights and data that they can use to tailor their coaching to individual needs. AI-powered coaching tools can analyze client data to identify patterns and trends, allowing coaches to make informed decisions about how to help their clients reach their goals. AI can also create personalized coaching plans considering individual learning styles, preferences, and strengths.

While VR and AI can potentially revolutionize the coaching world, they pose challenges for coaches and their clients. For example, some clients may feel uncomfortable using VR technology, while others may have concerns about using AI in their coaching sessions. Coaches may also need to invest

DOI: 10.4324/9781003439691-18

in expensive VR equipment and undergo training to use the technology effectively. However, the benefits of VR and AI in coaching far outweigh the challenges. Coaches who embrace these technologies can offer their clients a more engaging, effective, and personalized coaching experience, leading to better outcomes and improved client satisfaction.

14.1 Transforming Coaching Practices

In coaching, combining VR and AI has revolutionized how individuals receive guidance and improve their performance. Traditional coaching methods rely on subjective assessments and feedback, leaving room for interpretation and biases. However, VR and AI technologies provide a unique opportunity to measure performance objectively, offer targeted feedback, and create immersive coaching experiences that accelerate growth and development. This chapter explores how VR and AI can be leveraged to enhance coaching by measuring performance and delivering personalized feedback.

14.1.1 The Power of VR in Coaching

VR has emerged as a powerful tool for creating realistic and immersive environments, allowing individuals to practice and refine their skills in a safe and controlled setting. By simulating real-world scenarios, VR enables coaches to assess performance more accurately and objectively. Athletes can visualize themselves in competitive situations, professionals can rehearse challenging presentations, and individuals can face their fears in a controlled environment. Measuring and analyzing performance in VR provides valuable data that can be used to offer specific and targeted feedback.

14.1.2 AI: Unlocking Personalized Coaching

AI complements VR by analyzing vast data collected during VR simulations. Through machine learning algorithms, AI can identify patterns, evaluate performance metrics, and provide personalized feedback tailored to individual needs. Coaches can use AI-powered systems to track progress, measure key performance indicators, and identify areas for improvement. By analyzing data in real time, AI algorithms can identify nuances and provide insights that may be missed by human coaches alone, leading to more effective coaching outcomes.

14.1.3 Measuring Performance: Objective Assessments in VR

In traditional coaching, subjective judgments often play a significant role. However, VR offers the possibility of objective assessments by capturing and measuring various aspects of performance. Motion, eye-tracking, and biometric sensors can provide valuable data on body movements, gaze patterns, and physiological responses. AI algorithms can then analyze these measurements to provide quantitative feedback, eliminating biases and promoting accurate assessments. VR simulations allow for repeated practice and performance evaluation, enabling coaches to track progress and provide targeted interventions.

14.1.4 Personalized Feedback: Tailoring Coaching to Individual Needs

One of the primary benefits of combining VR and AI in coaching is the ability to provide personalized feedback. AI algorithms can analyze performance data to identify strengths and weaknesses, generating insights that inform tailored coaching strategies. Feedback can be delivered in real time during VR simulations or through post-session analysis, ensuring that individuals receive timely guidance to address their unique development areas. This personalized approach enhances coaching effectiveness, as individuals can focus on areas that require improvement.

14.1.5 Ethical Considerations and Human Intervention

While VR and AI have immense potential in coaching, it is essential to recognize the limitations and ethical considerations involved. The role of human coaches remains crucial in providing emotional support, building rapport, and interpreting complex human interactions that AI may struggle to grasp fully. Coaches must strike a balance between leveraging technology and maintaining a human touch. Ethical considerations around data privacy, consent, and the responsible use of AI must also be at the forefront to ensure the well-being and trust of individuals undergoing coaching.

VR and AI have opened up new avenues for coaching by enabling objective performance measurement and personalized feedback. The immersive experiences offered by VR provide a realistic training ground, while AI algorithms analyze data to provide valuable insights. The synergy between these technologies allows coaches to offer tailored guidance, track progress, and accelerate the development of individuals. As VR and AI continue to evolve, the coaching landscape stands to benefit from their integration, driving improved performance outcomes and transforming the way we approach personal and professional development.

14.2 Case Studies

This section will describe real projects and case studies applied to essential companies. The companies that will be mentioned are significant players in the international market, have collaborated with major companies, and, most importantly, are innovating the training and coaching industry with two of the powerful technologies of the future: VR and AI.

It may sound trivial, but before Meta invested billions in advertising, most people did not know VR and the metaverse. Thus approaching many curious people. The second aspect has given a boost to companies thinking of integrating new technologies, understanding, and having a clear vision. More and more companies are designing, testing, and implementing within their corporate training process.

Talespin published an interesting case study regarding leadership training in VR. A module in VR where one can train: advocacy, empathy, being present, probing questions, curiosity, flexibility, goal setting, motivating, cultural intelligence, and inclusivity.

PwC chose Talespin's CoPilot and Dashboard software platforms to help enable the VR portion of the study. CoPilot helps learners acquire and practice crucial soft skills in a secure and monitored environment by simulating genuine discussions in VR using AI and computer-generated people. The backbone for performance evaluation, skill analysis, and content distribution is the Talespin Dashboard.

PwC chose participants from a group of new managers in 12 PwC US locations to take the same unconscious bias training course in one of three learning modalities: classroom learning, e-learning, or a VR soft skills training course developed in partnership with Talespin. This study is the most significant investigation of VR soft skills training for large-scale enterprise deployment.

The study's findings demonstrated that VR could assist company executives in upskilling their workers more quickly, effectively, and affordably than alternative approaches, significantly when training resources may be decreasing and remote working may become more common (Talespin, 2023).

Another interesting case study is Bodyswaps, a project based in the UK.

Within the website, you can see some exciting case studies that can be highlighted.

According to the website:

> Bodyswaps is the most engaging, safe, and effective way for employees to train soft skills and bridge the ever-elusive gap between learning and workplace performance. We offer a library of off-the-shelf workplace simulations to practice communication and leadership skills in safe and realistic environments. All simulations are available for VR, PC, and mobile in English and French.

Listed here are some interesting case studies:

- Mental Health Nurse Training
- Performance Management Training
- Safeguarding Training
- Employability Training
- Diversity
- Healthcare

This is an additional project to consider and watch (Bodyswaps, 2022).

Last but not least, an interesting project to follow and look at is Vrainers, one of the first innovative e-learning apps on Meta Quest, that allows you to train your TEAM's soft and hard skills in VR and with the power of AI; also with branded and personalized simulations. Within the platform are different simulation programs: public speaking simulation and mindfulness.

Let us start with public speaking and pitch storytelling. It is much more prevalent today than expected; at least 1 in 3 people admitted to feeling uncomfortable. Talking with industry experts and professionals, it is realized how much this area lacked a "simulator" that would allow coaches and especially students to practice after a coaching session. Imagine we were having a coaching session to prepare an essential corporate presentation or a new project for investors. What are the most popular techniques today? The mirror, visualization, and the classic "grandmother" who can listen to us, but what is the commitment and mental effort they require? Plus, we do not consider the level of procrastination, a human aspect, but one that should not be underestimated, let alone disregarded. In this precise "gap" between coaching and performance, that VR with AI comes into play, that is, a virtual gym, where we can make mistakes, talk, fail, and try again without feeling the weight of constant judgment on our shoulders and be able to feel free to improve constantly. It may sound trivial, but solo training boosts our self-esteem and confidence and better prepares us by putting our coach's advice into practice. Coaching plays a key role, and one of the crucial premises is that these tools are not meant to go and replace them but to be a supportive tool, an accelerator of results and performance (Vrainers, 2023).

Last but not least, the coach will play a key role because they can remotely monitor the improvements of the person they are following and provide feedback remotely.

The e-learning platform brings several innovations and matches between the two emerging technologies:

- Introduction of a *virtual assistant* with whom to communicate vocally to manage content.
- Implementation of *realistic simulations* with high emotional impact. As seen previously in several chapters, emotional impact and the ability to trick our minds are vital pieces and advantages for those using immersive realities.
- *Speech generation* that can be edited, saved, and used for training. One aspect often underestimated is the ability to write a winning speech. Public speaking requires a significant commitment, so having a "helper" to write, edit, save, check, and use within simulations is a great winning strategy.
- Inclusion of *multiple languages* available to generate the pitch and dialogue with the virtual assistant. English now in the business world has taken an important position. Still, it is also true that organizing a speech first in our native language and then translating not only speeds up the speed of amplification with the text but also a more conscious choice of words.

Each pathway is designed not only to facilitate the student and expedite their training but also for the coach themselves to provide their students with their time and skills and a training tool that they can use unencumbered by their time and with the ability to monitor results.

References

Bodyswaps (2022). Bodyswaps®. Available at: https://bodyswaps.co/project/george -brown-college-dives-into-vr-interview-training-with-bodyswaps/.

Talespin (2023). Talespin. Available at: https://www.talespin.com/.

Vrainers (2023). Vrainers. Available at: https://vrainers.com/.

Chapter 15

Next Steps

In this century, robots will likely replace most of the jobs humans do (Ross, 2016). Hard skills used to be the only knowledge required, but in the last few years, soft skills are becoming more in demand.

With the advent and speed of how technology is developing, many subjects that we still study in schools and universities may no longer exist in the next few years. If we think about the most important leaders we have had in the past we identify specific characteristics, such as their ability to communicate. Names of great personalities such as Gandhi, Steve Jobs and so on come to mind, thanks to their charisma and communication skills. They were able to inspire the masses. These human capabilities cannot be replaced.

Let's get into the specifics by examining a speech made by Winston Churchill.

> Winston Churchill was asked to speak before a class of undergraduates at a prestigious military academy in the United States. He was asked to talk about success and how to achieve it. He approached the podium slowly but surely. At that time, Churchill was well advanced in years. He was pretty old.
>
> Not a fly was heard in the audience. Everyone understood this was a historic occasion. You could hear a pin drop on the carpet. Sir Winston reached the microphone, put down his cane, removed his top hat, adjusted his glasses, and glanced at the audience.

DOI: 10.4324/9781003439691-19

Then he approached the microphone and said three words: "Never give up." A long silent pause followed, and then, a few moments later, he repeated with the same calm: "Never give up." He looked again at his audience, and after a few moments of deafening silence, he said for the third time: "Never give up." Once he had said these words, he put his top hat back on his head, grabbed his cane, put his cigar between his teeth, and slowly but surely walked out of the stage along the central corridor, crossing the audience between two rows of seats. That performance is a clear example of strength with style. It takes pure, unadulterated confidence to do what Churchill did: say nine words at a graduation ceremony and then walk away. To do something like that, they have to feel good about themselves. Confidence is all about being comfortable with yourself in any situation. Having or not having confidence has nothing to do with what happens outside of us. Confidence is determined by what's going on inside you.

This talk can make us think about some critical issues. If self-confidence is purely personal, subjective, and intrinsic, how can machines replicate and create a sense of confidence? We are not talking about numbers, data, statistics, or anything else, but about experiences, mistakes, determination, courage and will to fight, values, beliefs, firm principles, and heart. In addition, even if we were to program a machine, the first thought is: Would it be able to make such a speech? Let us take a step back and think about where so much confidence and strength of these words come from. Many will be thinking first of all about the experience. Quite right. But going even more profound, it is the fruit and success of what Hayek saw for rules, that is, that today the laws that govern us are the best because they are the result of a constant selection over time, where it is the rule itself that corrects the direction. Therefore, his thoughts and words are the result not only of experience but also of emotions, of the meanings given to events, and his beliefs and values that have matured over time. Again, as anticipated in the introduction, we are discussing a futuristic vision of technology and VR, but it is time to start asking meaningful questions and reflections. We are not quite there yet, so we still have some essential advantages to hold on to.

According to Forbes, the hottest topics for the future of VR and AR are mainly focused on marketing and advertising. Think about the ability to promote a product through VR and AR, which can add value due to visualizations and experiences most relevant to sales and marketing processes. This can also facilitate new experiences and interactions with brands and products; with VR, you can have more individual experiences, and with AR, with more than one person. Also, you can create interactive experiences in the short term for storytelling. Thinking about augmented reality, you can personalize everything, and technology can influence: messages, colors, avatars, timing, and positioning. Exploring products will be our reality by creating more immersive experiences and getting a 360° view of the product, and e-commerce will gain.

Also, for these nonprofits that want to share their missions and in the gala dinner, they can showcase with AR the communities they serve, and with VR, you can experience the same journey to attend schools in Africa.

Getting into the metaverse, let us take what Travis Scott, an American rapper-singer, has accomplished digitally. On April 24, 2020, he launched his song through a digital and virtual event known as "Astronomical" at the Sweaty Sands, attracting over 12 million viewers within the video game Fortnite. This makes us wonder how much things could change, even how events and concerts are changing, and it is just the beginning (Barbera, 2020).

According to what was presented at GTC China 2018, most critical projects are conducted in the gaming and entertainment sectors, which are more commercial and can produce more profit in the short term.

So technology or technique is leading us toward progress, but we need to use our imagination to fully understand where a type of project can take us and be careful about the values we choose. There is still time.

15.1 A New Synergy

Using this way to train and increase your skills and knowledge can decrease the number of hours a trainer, coach, or manager has to spend on a new hire, and as a result, the process of independence at work will be much faster than before. AI has a critical feature that can also record and track improvements, so it cannot just be helpful as a monitoring tool. Also, what if the boss directly programmed the avatar based on the type of knowledge the worker should have? In addition, having the ability to more easily monitor, manage, and assess each person's growth and less complex management.

Another point that technologies cannot replicate is the synergy generated when a group of people comes together to create something more significant, also referred to by Napoleon Hill as the "alliance of brains" in his book

Think and Grow Rich. This principle describes the "coordination of effort and knowledge between two or more people, in a spirit of harmony and to achieve a goal." He continues, "When two minds come together, they always create a third, intangible and invisible force, which we can compare to a third, superior mind." A great example is provided by Peter Thiel when in the book *Zero to One* he describes the "Paypal Mafia," composed of Elon Musk, Reid Hoffman, Steve Chen, Chad Hurley, Jawed Karim, Jeremy Stoppelman, Russell Simmons, and David Sacks, names that have founded some of the most important companies of the last century (Thiel & Masters, 2014).

As written in the AI annual report 2018 by Francesca Rossi of the University of Padua, on AI, it is essential to move from human *vs.* machine to human *plus* machine to increase human intelligence.

Robots in the next year can be used to replace more than 800 jobs in the next 13 years. In the digital age, we must remain aware of technology integration, and workers must focus their skills to adapt and overcome the transformation. However, AI and robots lack soft skills such as leadership and charisma, and the only way to improve more than just businesses is through the human–machine relationship (Maccarrone, 2018).

IoT and AI can help humans learn more about the capabilities and applications of new digital technologies. Human–machine synergy begins when a company needs to provide higher customer satisfaction, which means optimizing resources, costs, and personnel. For example, a company can use refrigeration units to optimize generator operations in logistics processes, saving $6.5 million in one year.

However, there are also several limitations of IoT and AI. Undoubtedly, machines can only work and learn within a specific framework specified by an operator for a particular purpose, so all the information gathered will be in the hands of humans, who must make decisions. Also, it depends on the job whether to use IoT and AI or not; for example, if there is a case with a long job and raw data sets, it is possible to use them to optimize processes to find a solution quickly and save money.

In the book by Max Tegmark, *Life 3.0*, an analysis of various evolutionary steps taken so far is shown. *Life 1.0* reflects a world in which single-celled animals, protozoa, and amoebas could replenish themselves and seek food to survive. Then, in *Life 2.0*, humans and animals live together, and humans dominate the animals. Through culture and generation after generation, we have been able to modify and improve our behavior. Last but not least, *Life 3.0*, humans and robots, from cellular organisms to computers that can replicate and build. The topic of strong AI is described as having high potential and being virtually unlimited. In fact, in a hypothetical future, it will be crucial to hide it from the eyes of the world, but especially to disconnect it from the web world. One problem is related to the control of technology; probably at the beginning, we cannot see the effect of what we are doing, but before we learn to control and prevent certain situations, then we can better manage and understand how to deal with them (Tegmark, 2017).

Also, it might be relevant to reflect on the meaning of oneness for a human; for this, we can start from what Paul Coelho said, "The soul is our dwelling place; our eyes are our windows, and our words its messengers." The feelings and emotions a person can convey with their eyes are unique. However, in business, especially in education, growing a person to become more successful is based on the human. Thanks to investments and the fact that people work hard, technologies are developing so fast that we now have a choice: either use those technologies as a tool to create and help humans become better and better, or they will replace us.

Thanks to all the studies and reports, it is relevant to point out that an individual needs to develop some soft skills, not only for the benefits you can get in the workplace but also because improving that sense of leadership can be an advantage against any machine. What can make a human unique and cannot be replaced by a machine are characteristics such as charisma, leadership, communication skills, the determination that only a person can convey, and being able to inspire others.

The new skills we need to understand what is going on, but more importantly, to make qualitative and quantitative decisions for our future.

We have always talked about vertical skills, but in a fast-changing world, especially the technological world more than having technical skills is needed, as is having only business skills. We need a new key, something that not only gives us the ability to develop a business or grow a business concretely but also has less tangible aspects, such as philosophy, in terms of critical thinking, but helps us understand what principles to build or direct our business.

To summarize, starting from the research question, the book realized that these technologies can be applied to learning processes; however, there are some limitations to overcome, and in the next five to ten years, we will see the results. Humans have some unique characteristics; a machine or a robot cannot replace that, and we are responsible for developing them.

Steve Jobs said, "It's not a faith in technology. It's a faith in people." Like the entire historical period of innovation, what we do today is reflected in the future of the next generation.

References

Barbera, D. (2020). *12 milioni di persone hanno seguito il concerto virtuale di Travis Scott su Fortnite.* [online] Wired Italia. Available at: https://www.wired.it/gadget/videogiochi/2020/04/24/concerto-travis-scott-fortnite/.

Maccarrone, C. (2018). *Quali sono le soft skills da allenare per trovare lavoro.* [online] Forbes Italia. Available at: https://forbes.it/2018/02/17/quali-sono-le-soft-skills-da-allenare-per-trovare-lavoro/artificial-intelligence-memorial-roman-mazurenko- bot..

Ross, A. (2016). *The industries of the future.* New York: Simon & Schuster.

Tegmark, M. (2017). *Life 3.0.* New York: Alfred A. Knopf.

Thiel, P., & Masters, B. (2014). *Zero to one. Notes on startups or how to build the future.* Crown Currency.

Conclusion

We are at a very delicate moment in history. A technological revolution, ongoing wars, and having just fought against a pandemic, it is at such complex times that the decisions we make will be the foundation for our future. Among the speakers at a conference in Italy, one person expressed this exciting analysis: a driver's license is not given to everyone; it is hard to see a ten-year-old or a blind person driving a car. Likewise, understand what limits cannot be exceeded to use the potential of new technologies appropriately and safely. Will a license be needed? We will leave the word to experts in the legal and juridical spheres. Indeed, the case in Italy has begun to attract the attention of many countries, bringing a point of view other than simple enthusiasm for a technological novelty.

There is no doubt that the way companies are doing business is changing, and every entrepreneur, collaborator, and mainly students who want to understand and learn about these new technologies need multiple keys to interpretation: business and management, technological, philosophical, and psychological, as addressed in Chapter 7, Figure 7.1.

Thanks to a headset, VR is a technology that allows immersion in highly realistic virtual environments characterized by involvement, interaction, and participation, within which the user becomes an active creator of his own experience. It allows you to experience the so-called sense of presence: the person feels inside the occasion (being there) and, through specific commands, can interact with the scene in which he is. It is defined as a three-dimensional computer-generated environment in which the subject or subjects interact with each other and the environment as if they were inside it. Augmented reality is a technology that allows, through particular digital tools, to interact with the external environment. A straightforward example is augmented reality "experienced" through mobile devices. Nowadays, all smartphones and tablets have a camera, GPS, compass, and accelerometer,

DOI: 10.4324/9781003439691-20

allowing the user to view a series of data and information related to the area framed by the camera lens. Artificial intelligence belongs to computer science which studies the theoretical foundations, methodologies, and techniques that allow the design of hardware and software systems capable of simulating human performance. This last technology has existed for many years due to the complexity of managing it compared to virtual and augmented reality. Once presented with these innovative means, we tried to clarify the difference between artificial intelligence and human intelligence, focusing on the limits of the former in emulating the latter. Specifically, thoughts, compassion, and empathy are unique aspects of human intelligence and still difficult to insert them within simulation software. After this roundup of technological issues, we moved on to contexts closer to our daily lives, always focusing on the human–technology relationship. It presents how our habits have changed with innovation that advances through time management, workspaces, relationships, and ways of training mental skills and training. Specifically, how coaching pathways are and how they have evolved thanks to new technologies. We then analyzed soft skills and methods of enhancing them, comparing traditional and innovative methodologies. In particular, we focused on communication skills, stress management, and emotional intelligence, presenting this field's most used training methods and innovations.

Fundamentals skills are required to perform at a high level. That is true for business as for sports. For achieving our "peak performance," simple knowledge is not enough, the information is not enough, and what is asked to do goes beyond a reductionistic vision of performance.

One of the objectives of this book is to demonstrate the potential of new media, which at the same time can become barriers for those who interact with them. From the various studies presented, virtual reality, augmented reality, and artificial intelligence can be excellent support for training and coaching in business. Still, they must be used with caution and specific skills on the part of professionals. In the same way, technologies have led to extraordinary results in other fields, including those outside of psychology and philosophy. We like to see new technologies as an opportunity: this happens only if the professionals who use them have specific knowledge and skills, an appropriate approach to technologies, and particular attention to the dynamics typical of using a medium. If not, technological innovation can become an obstacle and a problematic enemy to manage. Technology, then, can be considered a bomb ready to explode: if it is used by the right people, with the right skills, and in the right way, it can be managed and prevented from exploding, leading to irreparable consequences.

We conclude with a take inside a book by Galimberti, an Italian philosopher, essayist, psychoanalyst, and journalist, in his book *The Myths of Our Time,* from the original one, *I miti del nostro tempo.*

> as Furio Colombo writes, "Technical progress is not always better, even if it is inevitable." And in front of the inevitable, to refuse is pathetic, but to watch is necessary, if only to understand, besides what we can do with technology, what technology has done, does, and will do with us even before we can do anything thanks to it.

We would like to conclude with a sentence that represents the vision of the book and the Vrainers project:

> Technology at the service of man and not a man at the service of technology.

The main objective of this writing has been to unite the worlds of innovation, economics, philosophy, and psychology.

Index

For Product Safety Concerns and Information please contact our EU representative GPSR@taylorandfrancis.com
Taylor & Francis Verlag GmbH, Kaufingerstraße 24, 80331 München, Germany

Printed in the United States
by Baker & Taylor Publisher Services